THE TRAGEDY
AT THE LOOMIS STREET CROSSING

The dramatic cover picture shows the extent to which the Exposition Flyer has buried itself inside the last car of the Advance Flyer. Photograph from May 2nd, 1946 edition of the Naperville Sun courtesy of Sun-Time Media.

Photograph appearing on this page and page 55 courtesy of Charles W. Cushman Collection: Indiana University Archives (P03246).

CHUCK SPINNER

AuthorHouse™
1663 Liberty Drive
Bloomington, IN 47403
www.authorhouse.com
Phone: 1-800-839-8640

Published by AuthorHouse 4/27/2012

ISBN: 978-1-4685-5594-3 (sc)
ISBN: 978-1-4685-5593-6 (e)

Library of Congress Control Number: 2012904250

Any people depicted in stock imagery provided by Thinkstock are models, and such images are being used for illustrative purposes only. Certain stock imagery © Thinkstock.

This book is printed on acid-free paper.

Because of the dynamic nature of the Internet, any web addresses or links contained in this book may have changed since publication and may no longer be valid. The views expressed in this work are solely those of the author and do not necessarily reflect the views of the publisher, and the publisher hereby disclaims any responsibility for them.

authorHOUSE®

This photo gives a clear picture of the accident scene. On the left (North) side of the railroad tracks can be seen Kroehler Furniture Factory and the Naperville water tower. On the right (South) side of the tracks is Fourth Avenue crossed by Loomis Street. In the intersection can be seen the engine of the Exposition Flyer imbedded in the last car #1376 of the Advance Flyer. Behind car #1376 and to the left is the slightly damaged second last parlor car, the Mississippi. To the right of the Mississippi is the nearly totally destroyed third last car, the Silver Inn dining car. To the right of the Silver Inn is the overturned Silver Cloud passenger car. Behind the Silver Cloud is the derailed Silver Gleam passenger car. The darken area, two car lengths east of the Loomis Street crossing next to the trees indicates the point of impact. Photo courtesy of Paul Hinterlong.

TABLE OF CONTENTS

DEDICATION

This dedication goes to a number of people:

1. The men, women, and children who died in the crash and the families that they left behind. Hopefully this book has revealed that the number dead were more than just statistics. These victims were people who were loved and cherished, and now more fittingly remembered.

    The passengers who survived the crash. Hopefully, their appreciation for an extended lease on life allowed them to produce greater positive effects on their communities than otherwise would have been their destiny. Any efforts in their extended lives made on behalf of the fallen victims of the wreck serve more a monument than ever could have been placed at the site of the crash.

2. All the Burlington Train employees who worked the rails and provided a vital means of transportation during and after World War II. In my research I hope that train enthusiasts look at the emphasis I've placed on this important rail event that for so long has been ignored by the general public. I hope I am forgiven if I have fallen short at times in meeting their standard of technical excellence in my explanations. Instead I hope they understand and appreciate my attempt to reduce, what can be at times very complex issues, into layperson terms. Special thanks in this regard goes to Rupert Gamlen who took my email questions and was able to elicit wonderful responses from former rail employees and rail enthusiasts Bob Webber, Bill Barber, Bob Campbell, Sam Cook, Pete Hedgpeth, Bob Dillon, Bryan Howell, Dean Houston, and others I'm sure I forgot to mention. Hol Wagner and J.W. Schultz co-edited a fantastic history of the Exposition Flyer (Burlington Bulletin, No.42, 2003) that was extremely helpful in my research.

3. The people who came to aid the victims of the crash. Those neighbors, Kroehler employees, Evangelical Theological seminary students, North Central College students, priests, firemen, police, ambulance workers, medical personnel, and even uninjured passengers from both trains who saw people in need and never hesitated in extending a hand. These were not the rubberneckers who at times clogged up recovery efforts, but people who came and stayed to help until either their bodies or the need for their help were exhausted.

4. Primary and secondary sources . The many people who have allowed me to interview them; who have sent me articles; and who have given me encouragement and support. I have printed

many of these names in the acknowledgment section. Their participation has enabled me to present their stories and those of so many others as accurately as possible. The support given by Bope Schrader is here singled out for special mention.

5. The many library and newspaper researchers and archivists, many of whose names are listed in the acknowledgment section at the back of the book, who so willingly used their time and talents to once again bring to light, stories that for 66 years had been forgotten. Special mention goes to Kimberly Jacobson Butler, North Central College archivist; the staff at the Chicago Public Library; and Bryan Ogg of the Naperville Heritage Society all of whom opened their archival files for my research.

6. Paul Hinterlong who graciously shared the many historical photographs of the crash site that he has purchased over the years.

7. My very talented nephew, JD Spinner who again created a fantastic cover for my second book; my good friend Rosemary Merchant who worked to proofread and clean up my manuscript; Jean McGowan for her computer expertise; AuthorHouse Publishing Company (especially J.R. Turner and his design team) for providing the avenue and assistance for putting this work into print; and friend Judi Goerke for her enthusiastic promotion of this work.

8. My wonderful wife, Patrice, who once again, as with my first book, showed me understanding and support, and allowed me the time and seclusion needed to produce both the research and the writing contained in this work.

9. Jim Christen, the premier expert on the technical aspects of the train wreck. Jim, unhesitatingly handed over the research he had accumulated for several decades on the Naperville train wreck. He was in communication with me throughout this long and involved project and painstakingly helped proofread the rough copies. Any credit in regard to the accuracy of the details of the wreck should go to Jim; any inaccuracies most probably fall to my misinterpretation of his research and documentation. More than anyone, he was my greatest asset and best supporter. This book was as much his dream as it was mine.

All that being said, I give a special dedication of the book to our two precious grandsons, Caleb and Joshua Spinner. I know they are proud of their Papa as he is of them. They are the light of their grandparents' lives. The boys' parents, Scott and Ellen, presented Patrice and me with two wonderful incentives to keep us vigorous in mind, spirit, and body so that we might share as much of their lives as the good Lord sees fit. Their smiles and unique personalities were an inspiration in my attempt to reproduce and restore to memory the individual lives of those who fell victim to the Naperville Train Wreck of April 25th, 1946.

Ex Burlington employee and rail history buff, Jim Christen with author. Picture taken by Tom Fitzgerald.

THE NAPERVILLE SUN   5c
Per Copy

Volume 11, Number 41   Naperville, Illinois,   Thursday, April 25, 1946

One of Worst Wrecks in Railroad History

REPORT NEARLY 100 KILLED IN TRAIN WRECK

*Haste in getting out the news of the tragic train wreck resulted in a number of
inaccurate statements. In their same day EXTRA edition, The Naperville Sun reported
what proved to be more than twice the final number of actual fatalities.*

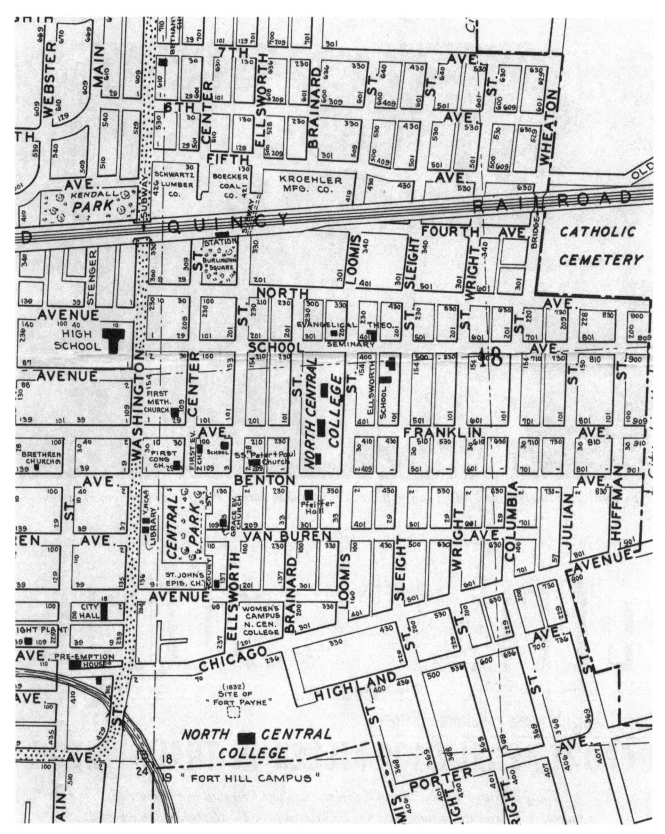

Map of Naperville detail from original drawn by Harold F. Steinbrecher, c. 1930. Courtesy of the Naperville Heritage Society.

INTRODUCTION FOR:
THE TRAGEDY AT THE LOOMIS STREET CROSSING

Travel

My heart is warm with friends I make,
And better friends I'll not be knowing;
Yet there isn't a train I wouldn't take,
No matter where it's going.
- Edna St. Vincent Millay

On April 25th, 1946, my mom was pregnant with me. In fact, she was at the end of her first trimester. I would be born on October 22, 1946. Our family lived in Naperville, Illinois, directly across from the main entrance of Kroehler Furniture Manufacturing Company, which at the time proudly displayed in big bold letters along the roof line of the building "World's Largest Furniture Manufacturing Company". Our house was on the north side of Kroehler; the railroad tracks ran along the south side. Our house was also just a block from the train intersection at Loomis Street.

At that Loomis Street crossing the most devastating railroad collision in the history of the Burlington railroad would take place. On that Thursday in April, at 1:05pm, the Exposition Flyer would ram into the back of the stopped Advance Flyer. The collision would result in 45 deaths and many more injuries.

The Kroehler building would shield our house from the site, but my brothers and sister could hear the wailing of the sirens for several hours as ambulances and support vehicles rushed to the scene. My brothers, John and Bob and my sister, Jean, were given strict instructions to stay in our house and not go to the tracks. Our mom, because of her pregnancy, was also kept from the scene. Our dad worked at Kroehler and like many of the 800 employees of the factory was at the site giving assistance.

The crash site was compared to a war zone. In fact, many soldiers who were returning from the war were passengers on those two trains. A number of them stated that they had been in combat situations, but that none of those battles had resulted in a scene as horrific.

After the bodies had been retrieved and sent to their various towns for burial, after the injured had been treated, and after the wreckage had been cleared away, not much was said or written thereafter about the Naperville train wreck of 1946. After my father died in 1961, I entered a boarding school seminary as a sophomore in high school. During my first day of class, each and every one of my instructors asked me to introduce myself to my new classmates. When I mentioned that I was from Naperville, inevitably the instructor would mention the association of my town with the 1946 train wreck. It was the first time I had heard of it. And, as I've found out, this omission was not too uncommon an occurrence.

Although some days are long, the years go by fast. I made the decision to leave the seminary after college. I then began a 33 year career teaching high school social studies in the Cleveland, Ohio area. That's where I met my wife, Patrice Supik and that's where we raised our son, Scott.

After I retired, I spent five years writing <u>A Book of Prayers: To the Heavens from the Stars</u> (abookofprayers.com), a collection of the beautiful favorite prayers from 118 wonderful celebrities. Then, one day as I was going through my files, I came across an article my mother had sent me some time before, that mentioned that it had been 40 years since the tragic Naperville train wreck. The article led to several reflections. My mother who had kindly sent me the article had died in 1998. The article reminded me of the many, many letters and articles she had sent her children during her lifetime. She was a wonderful, thoughtful mother and I always missed her, but the article especially focused my attention on her absence. The article also made me reflect on my father who had died at the age of 50. I was 14 years old at the time and thought of my father as an older man. However, now that I was in my 60s, I realized just how young he had been, and also how each day of my life is a precious gift to be used wisely. I've always been inspired by my dad who was a hard worker. On the day of the train wreck, workers at the nearby Kroehler Furniture Company were released from their jobs to help at the crash site. Although he never talked to me about that day, I'm certain that my father was one of the many who helped at the scene. After 25 years at Kroehler, our dad and his brother Bill bought the Naperville Liquor Store. Our dad could relate to all classes of people, and he loved his family dearly. His funeral was one of Naperville's largest.

Kroehler Furniture Ad from Chicago Daily News, April 26, 1946

Naperville Package Liquor Store ad from Naperville Sun, May 2, 1946.
Newspaper also references rescue worker Calista Wehrli.

The article also made me wonder why, after 61 years, nothing of any great substance had ever, to my knowledge, been written about the lives lost in that tragedy. Nor was there a monument or marker at the scene. I thought to myself, had those forty-five victims of the wreck all been from Naperville, there would have been any number of commemorative reminders of the lives that had been lost. The only reminder of the train wreck exists, not at the actual site, but at the Naperville downtown library. Outside the library, on its southeastern corner, there is a beautifully engraved casting of a map of the town. On that map there is depicted a train wreckage at the location where

the 1946 tragic accident took place. The number of dead listed on the casting is 47. My research findings concur with the original Interstate Commerce Commission's number of 45 fatalities.

I made a decision after looking at the article that I would begin research on the lives of those passengers and employees on the ill-fated trains who were victims of the crash. The book would be a long overdue commemoration of the lives filled with promise that were extinguished that day. More than that, I would try to present a

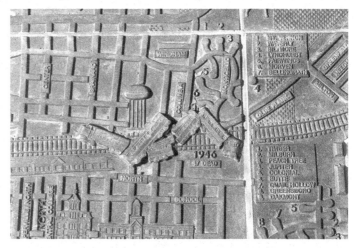

Section of engraved casting of Naperville map depicting 1946 train wreck. Map is located outside of Naperville's Nichols Library. Photograph taken by author.

picture of train travel coming to Naperville and the importance of the railroad as a stimulus to the city's tremendous growth. And I would investigate the causes of the crash, and try to explain these issues in layman's terms that could be easily understood. I would try to present a tribute to those who came quickly and stayed late to help those people who incurred injuries or death or who were just disoriented and wondering how they would complete their journey and how they would alert loved ones of their condition.

I don't know if my research will prompt a marker to be placed at the site of the tragic collision. I do hope that, at the very least, I can create in people a mental marker or monument that will now occupy a place in their conscious history of Naperville that was perhaps never there before.

Naperville was a great place to grow up – and it still is. The paper stand, Andy's Popcorn hut, and my dad and uncle's Naperville Liquor Store might no longer be there. But, SS Peter and Paul Church, the weekly band concerts, the beach, the "Roaring DuPage" River, the wonderful Memorial Day services and parade, and, of course the train depot will, I'm sure, long endure and are symbols of a large town that has managed to preserve its small town flavor. I am excited to be able to give something back to the town and the people who have given me and our relatives so much.

CHAPTER 1 -
TRACING THE PATH OF THE RAILROAD TO NAPERVILLE

Naperville High School Fight Song
All hail our school our NHS
We'll sing your praises, NHS
With all our might
we will always make a fight
to keep our standards high
for Naperville, so
give us a rousing cheer for Naperville
Our records must be fair
and bright, fair and bright!
So let us win today the
good ole way
It's up to you to fight, team, fight!
– Koerner
arr. Kaiser

The history of the growth and development of cities, towns, and villages in the United States can be generally traced to visionary pioneers and entrepreneurs, the community's accessibility to transportation systems, the genius of inventors, the growth and development of government documents and policies, and the determination of settlers focused on bettering their circumstances.

Naperville, Illinois is a suburb 28 miles west of Chicago. It presently covers 35.4 square miles and is the fifth largest city in Illinois with a population of 141,853 (2010 Federal Census figure).

This book is about a tragic train wreck that occurred in Naperville in 1946, a time when Naperville was a farm community of just over 5,000 residents. To be able to get a clear picture and an appreciation of the Naperville of 1946, one must first reflect back even beyond the community's beginnings for the reasons pioneers were inspired and motivated to migrate to Chicago and territories to its west. For an examination and understanding of Naperville's birth and development, we must go back East to our country's inception.

After the American Revolution and the defeat of the British, the fledgling United States during

1

the "Critical Period" certainly had its struggles. The country at this time was governed by the Articles of Confederation. This new government had to establish its power to tax, to make and enforce laws and to provide for the country's defense. It basically listed the elements that would be later displayed in a more organized and elegant fashion in our Constitution's Preamble. One of its biggest early challenges was the assimilation of new lands gained through war and eventually recognized by treaty and the growing power of our governments.

The first test involving the transfer of conquered lands into states took place in what was called the Northwest Territory. The lands of the Old Northwest included the land below the Great Lakes that was bordered on the west by the Mississippi River and on the east by the Ohio River.

At first there were overlapping claims on these lands by the eastern states of New York, Virginia, Massachusetts, and Connecticut. These states sought to extend their influence by extending the northern and southern lines of their latitudes into these new areas. When these states finally were persuaded to withdraw their claims, the strength and authority of the new central government was greatly enhanced.

One of the bright spots during the period that our country was ruled by the Articles of Confederation came with the passage of the Ordinances of 1785 and 1787. Basically, the 1785 Ordinance dealt with the way in which the new territories would be divided into five different entities. The 1787 Ordinance determined the manner in which these territories would be governed – first as territories, then as states.

Statesman Daniel Webster in 1830 had this to say in speaking of the impact of the Northwest Ordinance:

> "We are accustomed to praise the lawgivers of antiquity…but I doubt whether one single law of any lawgiver, ancient or modern, has produced effects of more distinct, marked, and lasting character than the Ordinance of 1787."

The new Northwest Territories were occupied by native American tribes, and Naperville's early history included very significant and frequent interactions with these peoples. Years later this influence could still be seen in the culture of the town. Naperville High School's sports teams in the 1940's were still called the "Redskins".

Obviously the Native Americans indigenous to the lands of the Old Northwest resisted the encroachment of the settlers into their territories. The Indians ultimately were subdued by war, much of their lands confiscated, and the Northwest Territory was effectively opened to settlement through the Treaty of Greenville (1795). As for the British, they finally were resigned to relinquish any claims and influence over these lands only after another conflict (War of 1812) and its subsequent treaty (Ghent 1815).

Finally, some form of peace and stability came to the Old Northwest and the flow of immigration into these territories began in earnest. The population requirement of 60,000 residents had been met by Ohio in 1803 and it became our country's 17th state. Now, quickly in succession, Indiana (1816) and Illinois (1818) entered the Union as well. The remaining two states fro the Northwest Territory,

Michigan and Wisconsin, would not meet the population eligibility requirement until 1837 and 1848 respectively.

A more temperate climate and the already existing Indian trails into these territories helped dictate that the southern three territories of the Old Northwest would be settled first with the population growth, of course, traveling east to west. It should be noted that settlement in the southern three states was also encouraged by the creation of the National Road which originated in Cumberland, Maryland in 1811 and would end up in 1839 in Vandalia, Illinois before construction stopped due to lack of further funding from Congress.

Another transportation innovation, the Erie Canal, opened in 1825 and facilitated travel for passengers and commodities from New York City to Buffalo and the Great Lakes. Governor DeWitt Clinton rode that first inaugural canal boat from Buffalo to New York City. That trip aboard the *Seneca Chief* took nine days and passed through 83 locks. On the boat were two barrels of water that were taken from Lake Erie and emptied into the Atlantic Ocean at the conclusion of the trip.

From Lake Erie, there were several options of travel out to the fertile lands of Illinois. The first of these options was overland travel.

The most prominent path through the Great Lakes region was the Great Sauk Trail created by Native Americans. This trail was in turn used by the French trappers, traders, and missionaries. In the early 1800's it was further developed as a military road that connected Detroit with Chicago's Fort Dearborn. The road was widened and graveled and known as the Detroit-Chicago turnpike or simply the Chicago Road. Chicago's Michigan Avenue was once part of the old Chicago Road.

Eventually the Chicago Road was used as a stagecoach route between Detroit and Chicago. Today, as part of the Interstate Highway System established during the Eisenhower administration, it is known as US 12.

Early settlers could also reach the new lands by water. From Lake Erie many early settlers sailed from Lake Erie to Lake St. Clair, up the St. Clair River, up through Lake Huron through the Straits of Mackinaw and down Lake Michigan to Chicago. Because of the ruggedness and dangers of land travel and the condition of the early roads, many people opted for lake travel. This avenue became even more attractive with the introduction of steamboats. This option was similar to the choice later gold rushers had to make between land travel across the continent or water travel around South America.

In fact, the lake route was the one Joseph Naper chose when he brought the founders of the Naper settlement from Ashtabula, Ohio. They traveled aboard the *Telegraph* and arrived at the new settlement on July 15, 1831. The *Telegraph* was a two mast schooner, with one deck, a scroll head, and a square stern. Naper, his wife Almeda Landon, and their family were aboard the ship. So was his brother John, his wife Betsy Goff, and their family. There were about thirteen families in all including Amy Naper and her husband John Murray, and the families of Lyman Butterfield, Harry Wilson, and Ira Carpenter. It's interesting to reflect now that at the time, the Naper settlement was on the fringe of the frontier of this country.

Naperville, of course, was named for Joe Naper. Although Naper was not the area's first European settler, he certainly earned the honor bestowed upon him. Joe and John Naper erected a sawmill within the first year of their arrival. Joe also was instrumental in establishing a trading post, a grist mill, and also helped establish the first school in the settlement. He was president of the first village council and helped lay out the road from Chicago to Galena.

The year after the Naper settlement was established, its livelihood was threatened by the outbreak of the uprising of the Sauk and Fox Indians in what was called the Blackhawk War. In 1830 President Andrew Jackson had signed the Indian Removal Act which called for the relocation of native Americans to west of the Mississippi River. Chief Keokuk and his followers acquiesced and moved west. Chief Blackhawk and his followers resisted and a short conflict ensued. Fort Payne was erected in the Naper settlement as a deterrent to possible attack; but before it was completed, most of the pioneers (1832 population = 180) fled for a short time to Fort Dearborn in Chicago for protection.

It is not surprising to learn that the county selected Joe Naper as captain of its first military organization. Fortunately, the Battle of Bad Axe (August 2, 1832) ended the Blackhawk War rather quickly. The Naper settlers never had to use their fort, and they were able to return from Chicago to the settlement and continue the growth and develop the history of their community.

DuPage County broke away from Cook County and became its own entity in 1839. Naperville was the oldest settlement in the county and became the county seat.

An interesting historical coincidence certainly helped the growth of this infant community transition from a settlement (1831) to a village (1857) and finally to a city (1890). The same year (1831) that the Naperville settlement was established, a Virginian named Cyrus McCormick was unveiling the mechanical reaper. His invention which eased the heretofore back-breaking process of harvesting wheat, earned for McCormick the title "Father of Modern Agriculture". William Seward, President Lincoln's Secretary of State (1861-1869) estimated that because of McCormick's invention of the reaper, "the line of civilization moves westward thirty miles each year." At the time of his invention, 90% of the population had been engaged in farming; eventually, because of industrialization, only 2% of the country's residents can now provide the food needs of a vastly greater population.

McCormick decided that Chicago would be the best location to build his reapers and so he moved there and built a manufacturing plant in 1839, the same year that Naperville was selected as the county seat for the newly incorporated DuPage County. McCormick's move to Chicago was very fortuitous, because before too long, Chicago became a railroad center that was able to transport crops harvested in the Midwest to consumers in both the East and the West. McCormick's organization would eventually grow into the McCormick International Harvester Corporation.

However, the presence of the railroad was still some years removed from the Chicago area. And, because of inventions like the reaper, growing farm communities like Naperville were faced with the problem of transporting an increased harvest to market. As necessity is the mother of invention, plank roads took the place of the previously very unworkable "corduroy" or log roads.

"Corduroy" roads were simply the laying of logs along the road perpendicular to the route of travel. The construction of the more durable and sophisticated plank roads involved generally a three stage process: the laying of planks perpendicular to the route of travel, the securing of three four-byfours as stringers on top of the planks, and then a final row of planks eight feet wide and usually two to three inches thick. . Even when the railroads were first brought to the Chicago area, farmers, for a time, still preferred plank roads or "farmers' railroads".

The Federal Land Act of 1841 was one in a series of land acts that provided an encouragement to settlers considering the move west. The act allowed heads of households, widows, or single men over 21 to buy up to 160 acres of land at $1.25 per acre. They could make this purchase after residing on the land for at least 14 months. Ten percent of the sale of the land went to the western states that made the sale. This act was fought by Easterners who were afraid of losing laborers.

To accommodate visitors to the settlement, hotels had to be built. The first hotel in Naperville; indeed, the first hotel in the lands west of Chicago, was the Pre-emption House. The structure served as a restaurant, boarding house, saloon, and stable. A lot of horse trading was done at the site. The Pre-emption House was torn down the same year as Naperville's tragic train wreck of 1946. The famous hotel stood at the corner of what is now Main Street and Chicago Avenue. The hotel had 19 guest rooms and was a stage coach stop for people traveling from Chicago to Galena, Illinois.

Ultimately, because of the various means of transportation and federal encouragements, over 200 wagons a day came to the Chicago area in the 1840's. Finished products were brought from the East and farm produce was sent back in return. From Chicago, roads were developed that led to Galena, Illinois and the Mississippi River.

Galena became a desired destination because of its fertile lands for farming and also for the abundance of lead to be found there. Galena, a name which is Latin for "sulphide of lead", was established in 1826. In 1845 Galena shipped a record 54,494,850 pounds of lead, and elaborate homes were being built in this city from the profits. The surface lead deposits were finally exhausted about the same time that settlers were enticed to travel all the way to the west coast in quest of another more precious mineral -gold- that was discovered at Sutter's Mill in 1848.

Ultimately, another man-made waterway, the Illinois and Michigan Canal, which was completed in 1848, connected Chicago with LaSalle-Peru on the Illinois River. At this point, travel by boat was possible from New York City all the way to the Gulf of Mexico. After the opening of the canal, the population of Chicago tripled in six years.

The prominence of the canal as a transportation link was short lived because of the influence of the railroads. By 1858 a railroad link from Chicago to New York City was established. The joining together of the Union Pacific and the Central Pacific in 1869 extended that rail route all the way to the Pacific coast.

The settlement of Naperville was, at first, very reluctant to join those villages that welcomed the railroad into their communities. The residents in 1851 refused to allow the Galena and Chicago Union Railroads to pass through their town. Thirteen years later Naperville realized that the future vitality of their community lay in the acceptance of rail transportation and a contract was signed in 1864 with the Chicago, Burlington, and Quincy (C,B,&Q). Unlike the pattern set by many of the other western suburbs along the C,B,&Q route to Chicago, the train did not pass through the center of Naperville. Those communities where the railroad dissected their town needed duplication of city resources to service both sides of town in case of a stopped train. Naperville's leaders wisely demanded that the Burlington railroad build their line on the northern border of the town. This provision necessitated a curve to swing the rails back to what was then the edge of town. In retrospect, this decision has provided modern Naperville with a more efficient traffic flow. However, as the reader will come to see, this curve in the line also certainly played a major role in the 1946 train wreck.

The Naper Settlement (pop. 2,000) gained the status of "village" in 1857 and it was more than appropriate that Joe Naper was named first president of the village council. Naper's oath of office, which follows in part, was much different than those taken today. "I…do solemnly swear…that I have not fought a duel, nor sent, nor accepted a challenge to fight a duel…since the adoption of the Constitution, and that I will not be so engaged or concerned, directly or indirectly…during my continuance in office…" (p134 "DuPage County, a descriptive and historical guide" edited by Marion Knoblauch, 1948).

In 1867 a referendum proclaimed that Wheaton, which was more centrally situated, would become the new county seat. Proud Naperville settlers were reluctant to hand over government documents and to relinquish this political distinction. Therefore, in 1868, in a night time raid, forty daring Wheaton residents took it upon themselves to break into Naperville's county office and abscond with the records. One of the items that was taken was a little brass bell. And, today the colleges of North Central of Naperville and Wheaton College play their annual football game for the honor of taking home that same "little brass bell".

In the 1860's, although Naperville lost the county seat, it gained a college. In 1861 the Evangelical Association established Plainfield College in the community of Plainfield, nine miles south of Naperville. The college trustees went to a more dignified name of North-Western College in 1864. In 1870 the Board of Trustees of North-Western College voted to move their facility to Naperville because of its greater accessibility to rail transportation. And in 1926 the Naperville trustees changed the name of their institution of higher learning to its current designation of North Central College.

One of the few classes available in the early days of the college was German language class. Many of Naperville's earliest settlers came from Germany. Some of them were experts at the handling of explosives and cutting limestone, skills needed in working the Naperville quarries. These quarries provided stone for Naperville's college and downtown buildings. The railroads carried the quarried stone that was in great demand in the rebuilding of Chicago structures destroyed in the devastating fire of October 8th, 1871.

The railroads early on had a great influence on the town of Naperville, and moreover, all of Illinois. Railroads allowed for the creation of suburbs, the transportation of grains and beef from west to east, the creation of catalog companies such as Montgomery Ward and Sears, and ultimately for attempts at state and federal regulation of railroad abuses. Illinois, with Chicago in particular being the hub of rail service at the time, was also the center of the industry's contentious litigation. The Illinois Granger Laws of the early 1870's were established to curb the abuses of the railroads, especially in regard to excessive grain storage rates. In 1877, the Supreme Court case of Munn vs. Illinois supported the Granger Laws; while in the 1886 Wabash Case, the Court stated that only Congress had the power to regulate interstate commerce. Because of all the problems between the farmers and the railroads, the federal Interstate Commerce Commission was established in 1887 to investigate and regulate the railroads.

Carl Sandburg who won Pulitzer Prizes in both history and poetry was from Galesburg, Illinois, a major rail center. Sandburg's father was a railroad blacksmith's helper and Carl spent some time in his youth riding the rails as a hobo. In his series of "Chicago" poems Sandburg noted Chicago's connection with the railroads when he wrote:

"Hog Butcher for the World, Tool Maker, Stacker of Wheat, Player with Railroads, and the Nation's Freight Handler, stormy, husky, brawling, City of the Big Shoulders."

It was appropriate that another big historical event both took place in Chicago and was initiated by the influence of the railroads. Again, if necessity is the mother of invention, then the railroads were the cause in 1883 of the standardized time system that was established to coordinate train schedules. Up until that time cities had simply fixed "noon" as the time when the sun was directly overhead. The new system suggested that if there are 360 degrees in a circle (earth), then a day (24 hours) would divide that circle into 24 equal time zones of 15% each. The United States, according to the new system, would consist of four time zones. On November 18th, 1883, when the system was officially initiated, Chicago lost 9 minutes and 33 seconds at 11:45am. With the new system, trains would run on time and a new order of efficiency was established, not only for the railroads, but for the general culture as well.

The turn of the century saw the start of a modern age that introduced the conveniences of water towers, sewers, electricity, and telephones to Naperville. My grandmother, Lena Riedy Rechenmacher once told me about neighborhood residents gathering in the road to watch the illumination of the first street lights in Naperville. She also reminisced about the first phone call her family made. After that phone call to the neighbors they all met in the street to marvel that "it sounded just like you. We just knew it was you!"

One of the big players in the train wreck of 1946 was the furniture factory, Kroehler, that was immediately adjacent to the north site of the wreck site. That furniture factory was first known as the Naperville Lounge Company when it was established in 1893. In 1902 Peter E. Kroehler bought the company. After the original building was devasted by a tornado in 1913, a new structure was built that was called the Kroehler Furniture Manufacturing Company. Like many manufacturing concerns, Kroehler discontinued specializing in the production of wooden lounge chairs and upholstered furniture during World War II. Instead, the company retooled to manufacture furniture and filing cabinets for U.S.O offices, duffel bags, airplane propellers, and even prosthetic limbs for soldiers. Kroehler was built right along Naperville's rail lines and the trains brought lumber and materials into the plant and shipped finished products to an almost inexhaustible market. At the time of the April 25th, 1946 train wreck (approximately 1:05 pm) the company suspended work for the rest of the day and many of the company's 800 workers quickly came to the aid of the victims of the crash.

At the time of the 1946 train wreck Naperville had no hospital that could treat injured passengers; however, there was a tuberculosis sanatorium that had been founded in 1907. Fire destroyed the main building in 1920. The building was restored and improvements made in the 30's due to the efforts of Joy Morton, owner of the Morton Salt Company. Joy Morton also created the renowned Morton Arboretum in neighboring Lisle, Illinois. This interest in trees was not unexpected as Joy's father, J. Sterling Morton, was the founder of National Arbor Day.

Once one of the leading causes of death in our country in the early 1900's, tuberculosis was able to be better controlled by the discoveries of streptomycin in 1944, aminosalicylic acid in 1949, and isoniazed in 1952. With the consequent decrease in the cases of tuberculosis, Edward Sanatorium was able to be converted into Edward Hospital in October of 1955, again, too late to be of help to the victims of the 1946 train wreck.

The growth of the Chicago, Burlington, and Quincy Railroad (CB&Q) mirrored that of Naperville. In 1864 when the CB&Q first came through Naperville, the line had 400 miles of track. In 1865 the Burlington was the first train line to run to the Union Stock Yards. Three years later the CB&Q had spanned bridges over the Mississippi River both at Burlington, Iowa and at Quincy, Illinois. The CB&Q assimilated several western rail lines and by 1882 was able to claim a direct line from Chicago, Illinois to Denver, Colorado. Because of the train line's reliance on farmers both as a supplier and recipient of goods, the company provided advice to prospective farmers who came out West. Before long, the CB&Q became known as a "Granger Railroad".

At the beginning of the 20th century, railroad magnate James J. Hill purchased control of the CB&Q. Hill's railroads, the Great Northern Railroad and the Northern Pacific consequently bought up 97.2% of CB&Q's stock. This event would play a part in the 1946 train wreck. The last car on the Advance Flyer (car #1376) was an older car borrowed on a per diem basis from the Northern Pacific Railroad.

Nearly all city to city passenger travel, from the middle 1800's until approximately 1920, was by railroad. However, due to the rise in popularity of the automobile, passenger rail travel declined drastically from 1920 to 1934.

During the Great Depression, many of the major railroad companies found it difficult to stay financially solvent. For instance, an indication of the financial troubles faced by the Denver and Rio Grande Western Railroad is shown by the acronym often assigned to them at the time - "Dangerous and Rapidly Getting Worse".

The U.S. Secretary of the Interior encouraged passenger train travel in order to keep the struggling rail industry from collapsing.

It might be surprisingly then to learn that the Burlington ascendency in the railroad industry came during these same hard economic times. Its rise has often been traced to one event and two men. The event was Chicago's 1933-34 Centennial celebration formally entitled, "A Century of Progress". The two men, Ralph Budd and Ed Budd, though they shared the same last name, were unrelated.

Burlington's locomotives had gone through an evolution of steam engines, powered first by wood and then by coal. Ralph Budd was the President of the Chicago, Burlington, and Quincy Railroad (commonly referred to the CB & Q, the Burlington, or simply the "Q"). In the first year of Chicago's centennial celebration (1933), Ralph was inspired by the diesel engine he saw exhibited at the fair. By the second year of the celebration (1934), Ralph Budd had combined a diesel engine with a unibodied stainless steel streamlined car designed by Ed Budd. The result was the Burlington Zephyr. "Zephyrus" was the god of the wind and a symbol of rebirth. Budd chose a name that started with a "Z" because he wanted it to be the "last word" in train design and technology.

The Union Pacific actually also came out with a type of diesel powered train, the M-10000 a couple months before the completion of the Zephyr. Both trains had streamlined articulated (two cars on one set of trucks, i.e., wheels) designs and huge followings at each of their appearances. However, it was the more superior technological advances of the Zephyr that made it ultimately prevail over the M-10000 which was retired in 1940.

To promote the Zephyr, Ralph Budd made the claim that his new train could travel non-stop all the way from Denver to Chicago, a distance of 1,015 miles. The longest previous non-stop travel by rail had been 775 miles. In addition, Ralph boasted that this first Zephyr, which he later called the Pioneer Zephyr, would cut the time for the distance traveled from 26 hours to 14 hours. The train's historic dawn-to-dusk run took place on May 26, 1934.The Zephyr actually covered the distance non-stop in 13 hours and 10 minutes! The train's arrival at Chicago's Century of Progress exhibit was greeted by a crowd of 100,000! The engineer for the historic run was Jack Ford who was born and raised in Aurora, Illinois. Aurora is seven miles west of Naperville.

The diesel powered train's average speed for the distance was 77.6 mph – its top speed, 112.5mph! Later that same year, the Pioneer Zephyr starred in the film Silver Streak. The film told the fictional story of a life saving run by the Pioneer Zephyr (renamed the Silver Streak for the film) to get an iron lung from Chicago to Boulder, Colorado in time to save the polio stricken son of the president of the railroad (In 1976 a comedy/thriller film also named Silver Streak, was produced starring Gene Wilder, Richard Pryor, and Jill Clayburgh). The Pioneer Zephyr can still be seen today at Chicago's Museum of Science and Industry.

So, actually, the two Budds would both play important parts in the Naperville crash of 1946. Ralph's emphasis on incorporating diesel engines that emphasized greater speed and Ed's protective stainless steel frames certainly can be said to have affected the Naperville crash in different ways.

The Naperville Country Club golf course is positioned south of the curve that brings rail traffic to and through Naperville. In the Fall of 1936 a four person film crew in a trim red Lockheed Vega airplane tried to take aerial publicity photographs of the BC&Q Zephyr as it rounded the bend coming into Naperville. The pilot lost control of the plane which crashed on the country club's fifth fairway. All four passengers (the pilot, two commercial photographers, and a script writer) died in the crash.

The surge in rail travel brought on by the diesel engine and streamlined cars was short lived and the depression once again dealt a blow to this industry until World War II.

Adolf Hitler's aggressive actions in Europe in the late thirties began to reignite the U.S. economy. U.S. industrial plants started to churn out war related products as the country's policies escalated from Cash-Carry to Lend-Lease. As a result, increased family incomes made possible the thought of family vacation rail travel.

In 1939, the United States hosted two world fairs – one in New York City and one in San Francisco. San Francisco's event celebrated the dedication of the SanFrancisco – Oakland Bridge in

1936 as well as the dedication of the Golden Gate Bridge in 1937. The Fair was called the Golden Gate International Exposition and was held on Treasure Island, which afterward was converted into a naval base. To take advantage of this attraction, the CB&Q in conjunction with the Denver & Rio Grande Western Railroad and the Western Pacific Railroad inaugurated the decade long run of the Exposition Flyer. The "Expo" was a diesel train with heavyweight equipment that ran between Chicago and Oakland. The Exposition Flyer was also known as train #39 for the year (1939) of San Francisco's Exposition. Rail experts and authors J.W. Schultz and Hol Wagner in their 2003 Burlington Bulletin #42 describe the fanfare that accompanied the inaugural journey of the Exposition Flyer:

"The premier departure of the west-bound Exposition Flyer from Chicago Union Station 35 minutes after noon on Saturday, June 10, 1939, was made an occasion of celebration that included music and brief speeches, in a unique christening ceremony in which five of the Exposition Flyer's young onboard hostesses – representing Miss Chicago, Miss Denver, Miss Salt Lake City, Miss Feather River Canyon, and Miss Treasure Island – used gilded hammers to smash a bottle containing water from San Francisco Bay, the Feather River, the Great Salt Lake, the Colorado, Missouri, and Mississippi Rivers and Lake Michigan. Providing music for the auspicious occasion was the Aurora (Illinois) East High School Band (playing 'California, Here I come') and the Pullman Porters' Quartet."

The very first passenger aboard that inaugural run was Charles Loesch. As a commemorative souvenir, hostess Evelyn McMannon presented Loesch with one of the ball peen hammers used in the Exposition Flyer's christening.

Most train lines have what is called a "drumhead". A drumhead is a logo that is featured on advertising, stationery, dining car menus, and often could be found as an electrically lit sign attached to the rear car of the train. In the case of train #39, the drumhead was round with the name Expostion Flyer superimposed over a picture of the Tower of the Sun. This tower, designed by Arthur Brown Jr., stood 392 feet tall and was the central feature of the Golden Gate Exposition. Each of the Exposition Flyer drumheads was unique as it was individually hand painted at the Burlington rail shop in Aurora, Illinois.

The bombing of Pearl Harbor and America's entrance in World War II would bring a resurgence to rail traffic due to the handling of troop movements as well as the restrictions placed on the production of automobiles and the rationing of gasoline. During the war, each day 300 trains passed through Chicago's Union Station which daily serviced 100,000 passengers.

The drumhead for the #39 Exposition Flyer featured the Tower of the Sun, the central feature of the 1939 Golden Gate Exposition. Each Expo drumhead was individually hand painted in the Aurora, Illinois rail shop. Printed courtesy of Duane Henry and Tomar Industries.

CHAPTER 2 – THE ROAD NOT TAKEN

<u>The Road Not Taken</u>
*Two roads diverged in a yellow wood,
And sorry I could not travel both
And be one traveler,
     long I stood
And looked down one as far as I could
To where it bent in the undergrowth.*

*Then took the other, as just as fair,
And having perhaps the better claim
Because it was grassy and wanted wear,
Though as for that the passing there
Had worn them really about the same.*

*And both that morning equally lay
In leaves no step had trodden black.
Oh, I marked the first for another day!
Yet knowing how way leads on to way
I doubted if I should ever come back.*

*I shall be telling this with a sigh
Somewhere ages and ages hence:
Two roads diverged in a wood, and I,
I took the one less traveled by,
And that has made all the difference.*
– Robert Frost

*"One thing about trains...it doesn't matter where they're going.
What matters is deciding to get on."
from Polar Express*

"The only way of catching a train I have ever discovered is to miss the train before.
- Gilbert K. Chesterton

The very last car, #1376, on the Advance Flyer was a consist (i.e. car) borrowed from the Northern Pacific line. The car would be removed from the Advance Flyer at Burlington Iowa and the passengers from that car heading further south of Burlington would then be put on the Mark Twain Zephyr. That train would head for towns such as Keokuk, Iowa; Fort Madison, Iowa; and Quincy, Illinois.

All of the people who will be mentioned in this section had originally intended on traveling aboard the Advance Flyer and would have been seated in car #1376. Had their intentions been carried out, nearly all of these people would have been killed or maimed little over one half hour into their journey.

There were, it seems, an equal number of persons who either originally did not intend on traveling on April 25th, or who were planning on traveling by some other means, who ultimately ended up on the fated Advance Flyer.

Since World War II had just recently ended, there were a good number of soldiers and sailors aboard the two trains. Sergeant Ned B. Gorrell had just been discharged from the army after his tour of duty in Japan. Gorrell was the son of Mrs. Betty B. Gorrell of Burlington, Iowa and the sergeant and his wife were in Chicago the morning of April 25th, 1946. They intended on taking the Advance Flyer to complete their trip home to Burlington. The couple were so anxious to get home that they decided instead to take the earlier 9:05am train out of Chicago. However, not having been informed of this change in plans, and having heard about the crash, Gorrell's mother was at the Burlington, Iowa station frantically awaiting the Advance Flyer's scheduled 3:42pm arrival.

Robert Ludford, a student from Iowa Wesleyan College, was on break and had just completed a visit to his home in Chicago. Ludford had planned on taking the Advance Flyer to Burlington and from there he would travel the remaining miles back to his college campus at Mt. Pleasant. Robert must have been a bit put out on Thursday morning when a longer than expected wait at a doctor's appointment forced him to make connections on a later train.

Gloria Echler was also a Wesleyan student on break in Chicago. An illness forced Gloria to postpone the trip back to campus that she originally would have made on the Advance Flyer.

Buffalo, New York residents Dr. and Mrs. E.A. Mathews planned on coming to Mt. Pleasant, Iowa to visit their daughter. Undecided as to whether to drive or go by train, at the last moment they chose to make the trip by car.

Couples, Mr. and Mrs. E.R. Busby and Mr. and Mrs. William J. Flynn, both were from Quincy, Illinois and both couples had been visiting friends in Chicago. For some reason on April 22nd the Busby's canceled their reservation on the Advance Flyer. Instead, they took the later train, the American Royal. Mr. Flynn's activities also necessitated a slight delay in Chicago and so that couple too was forced to take the later American Royal back to Quincy.

Yet another Quincy resident, Bernice Gottreu, recent graduate of St. Mary's hospital school of nursing was believed to have had reservations on train #11. However, she too, for reasons unknown, took the American Royal back to Quincy.

Elmer Sturhahn, a foreman at the Gardner-Denver plant in Quincy, Illinois intended to take train #11 from Chicago to Burlington, Iowa and then on to Quincy via the Mark Twain Zephyr. However, a friend who offered to make Sturhahn's reservation, booked a reservation on the American Royal instead of the Advance Flyer.

Monsignor Bernard J. Sinne of St. Mary Magdalene's Church of Omaha, Nebraska was scheduled to return to his home parish on the Advance Flyer. After news of the crash, a priest friend from Chicago, Father Leo McNamara came to St. Charles Hospital in Aurora looking for his friend and associate. Again, for some undetermined reason, Monsignor Sinne had returned to Omaha on another train.

The people we just mentioned, many would say, were given extensions to their lives. In like manner, modern medical advances have prolonged the lives of people who, had they lived in former generations, would have died from the diseases or conditions for which they are now successfully being treated. It's interesting to speculate if these fortunate circumstances granted randomly to certain individuals generally alter these persons' lives for the better. The probability of a positive change in character, outlook, and achievement is in most cases determined by whether each individual brought the fortuitousness of their situation to the level of consciousness over a prolonged period of time. It is hoped that these people realized that for whatever reason, their lives were spared. We hope that these survivors perhaps were more cognizant of their opportunity to make a positive effect on their community with the gift of time that they had been granted. In turn, perhaps they became more dedicated and determined to make up for the life opportunities denied to others due to an unforeseen set of tragic circumstances.

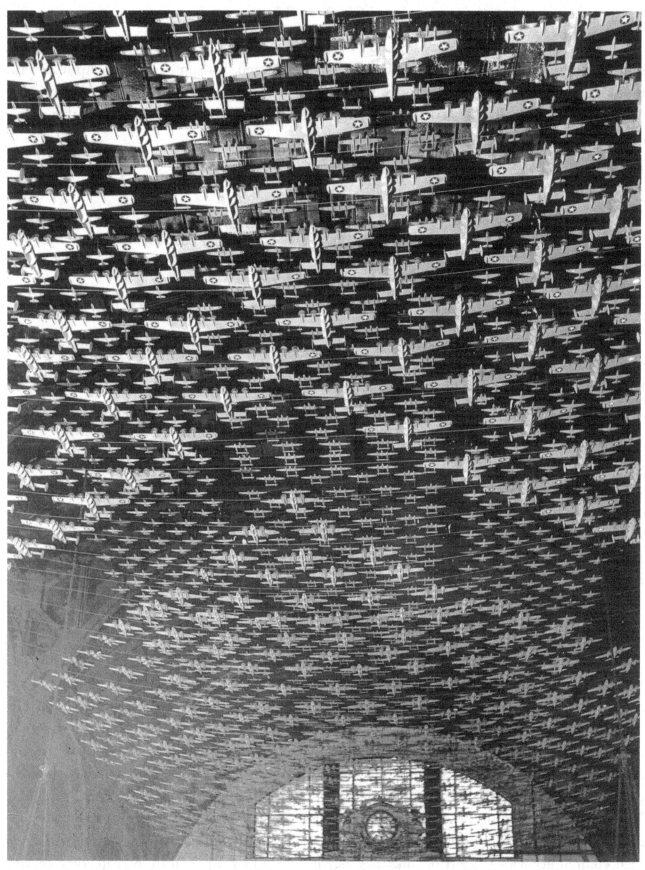

Passengers boarding trains at Union Station on April 25, 1946 looked in awe at the site of 4,500 model planes suspended thirty feet from the ceiling of the main concourse. Photograph from author's collection.

14

CHAPTER 3 - BOARDING THE TRAIN

In the late morning of April 25th, 1946, rail travelers and their loved ones who were seeing them off, started to arrive at Chicago's Union Station. A great number of the train passengers in this story were from Midwestern rural areas. Certainly most of them had to be greatly impressed when entering the huge concourse of Union Station, not only by the massive architecture of the structure, but also with the mass of humanity scurrying every which way within its confines. The station, which opened in 1925, took eleven years to build at an estimated cost of anywhere from 50 to 100 million dollars. Commuters passed under sky lighted 90 foot high ceilings in the main concourse. Suspended 30 feet from the ceiling were 4,500 scale model airplanes. There were also 12 large wartime murals hung from the walls. In the main concourse area Henry Harringer had created two 40 foot high murals. The first was an illustration of war bonds floating down over our nation's capitol. The second showed bombs falling upon the axis powers. In the waiting room there were ten additional large murals. Eight of these were pictures of heads of military personnel in the form of a soldier, a sailor, a marine, an aviator, a coast guardsman, merchant seaman, a Red Cross nurse, and a WAC. In addition, artist Gustav Rehberger had created two 30 foot murals. The first was labeled "Labor – we produce" while the second was titled appropriately, "Railroads – we produce". The presence of these murals had encouraged the wartime sale of bonds and war stamps. Passengers waited for their trains in the main waiting room that featured pink Tennessee marble floors and big wooden benches. Indeed, for our travelers, the Union Station must have seemed like an awe inspiring destination as well as a place of departure.

The majority of these passengers today were traveling for two reasons: some of them were returning from Easter visits to loved ones and some of them were soldiers and sailors either having been recently discharged after World War II or being on break from some branch of the Service.

The 1946 Christmas movie, <u>The Best Years of Our Lives</u> won seven Academy Awards for its depiction of the lives of three men returning home from military service after World War II. It was the highest grossing film of the decade. The idea for the movie came from a 1944 Time magazine photograph that showed a number of Marines on furlough looking out from a train car.

One might have had the mistaken assumption that the emotions of these men returning home after years at war would be ones of total elation. However, director William Wyler's film clearly portrayed the complex feelings of joy, confusion, and uncertainty occupying the minds of his three main characters: a former bombardier, an infantry sergeant, and an injured navy seaman who was returning home with prosthetic hooks as hands.

In writing this book on the Naperville train wreck, I soon realized that many of the passengers on both trains were also recently discharged or soon to be discharged military personnel. The servicemen on the Expo and Advanced Flyer obviously faced the same uncertainties as those soldiers portrayed by the actors in the aforementioned film. It was both coincidental and instructive to this author to learn that the film debuted the same year as the Naperville train wreck.

The passengers we're concerned with in this story were waiting to board one of two Burlington trains: the #11 (the Advance Flyer); or the #39 (the Exposition Flyer). Both trains were scheduled to depart from Union Station at 12:35pm. The passengers who got on car #1376, the last car of the Advance Flyer, were headed for Burlington, Iowa. At Burlington, all passengers would disembark from that car which was then released from the main body of the Advance Flyer. Those people headed for points south would board the Mark Twain Zephyr. Passengers in the other coach cars of #11 were staying on until Omaha or Lincoln Nebraska. The end of the line for passengers intending to take the Exposition Flyer, was Oakland, California. Our nation had just emerged from the end of World War II and the Advance Flyer gave evidence of the influence of that confrontation. The roofs of several of its stainless steel cars (eg. Silver Gleam and Silver Cloud of the Advance Flyer) had been painted black for camouflage wartime effect.

Passengers on the Advance Flyer whose destination was Lincoln or Omaha, Nebraska were seated on either the Silver Gleam (5th car from the rear) or the Silver Cloud (4th car from the rear). The third car from the rear was the dining car, the Silver Inn. The car immediately in front of #1376 was a parlor/observation/buffet car, the Mississippi. The Mississippi had just three months earlier come out of the Aurora shops after reconversion from its use as a military personnel carrier during the war.

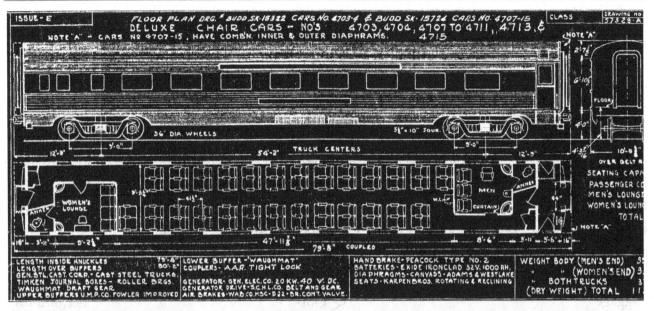

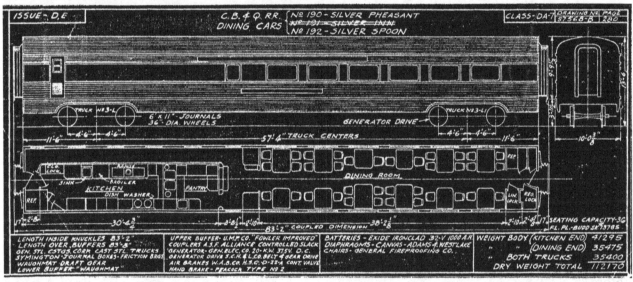

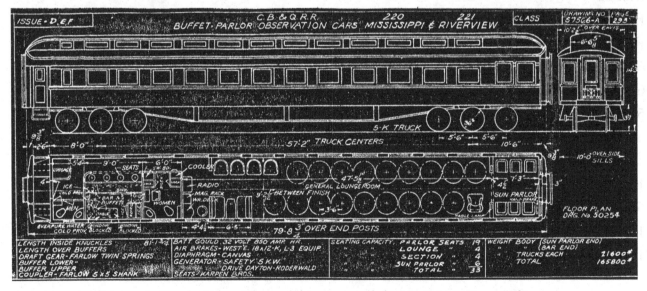

Schematics for the Silver Gleam, Silver Inn, and the Mississippi. From "Chicago, Burlington, and Quincy Passenger Car Diagram Book – 1949".

The consists (cars) for both the Advance Flyer and the Exposition Flyer are listed in the following charts:

No. 11 Advance Flyer

Type	Name	Length	Weight
motors (E7-E7)	Q 9920A-B		
baggage	UP 1652	60'	
postal storage	UP 2033	60'	
baggage-express	SP 6520	70'	
baggage	Q1317	60'	
60' Railway Post Office	Q 2326	60'	
express refrigerator	NYC 5963	54'	
baggage	Q 1586	70'	141,800 lbs
baggage	Q1564	70'	139,700 lbs
52-seat chair car	Q Silver Gleam	79'8"	110,700 lbs.
52-seat chair car	Q Silver Cloud	79'8"	112,950 lbs.
36-place dining car	Q Silver Inn	83'2"	115,800 lbs.
Buffet-parlor-solarium- observation care	Q Mississippi	81' 1 3/4"	169,800 lbs.
68-seat coach	NP #1376	79' 8 1/2"	169,300 lbs.

No. 39 Exposition Flyer

Type	Name
Motors	
E5A	Q 9910A Silver Speed
E5B	Q 9910B Silver Power
64-seat chair car	Q 4500
63-seat chair car	DRGW 961
57-seat chair car	DRGW 971
36-seat place dining car	Q 172
16-section tourist Pullman sleeping car	Pullman 4109
13-section tourist Pullman sleeping car	Pullman 1479
6-section/6-double bedroom sleeping car	Pullman Poplar Branch
10-section/1-drawing room/2-compartmen sleeping car	Pullman Lake Baron
10-section lounge- observation	Pullman Mt. Darwin

You will notice that train #39 contained two diesel engines and nine cars; while train #11 contained two diesel engines and 13 cars. This is opposite of what was reported in many newspaper accounts immediately after the train wreck.

THE CREW FOR THE ADVANCE FLYER

Engineer:	A.W. Anderson	Galesburg, Illinois
Fireman:	G.A. Abrahamson	Galesburg, Illinois
Conductor:	J.E. Aue	Rockford, Illinois
Brakeman:	S. Grant	Chicago, Illinois
Flagman:	J.J. Tangney	Aurora, Illinois

THE CREW FOR THE EXPOSITION FLYER

Engineer:	W. W. Blaine	Galesburg, Illinois
Fireman:	C. H. Crayton	Galesburg, Illinois
Conductor	G.W. Hill	Burlington, Iowa
Brakeman:	B.V. Landon	Galesburg, Illinois
Flagman:	C.W. Norris	Burlington, Iowa

PASSENGERS ON ADVANCE FLYER – NORTHERN PACIFIC CAR #1376

A recently discharged Marine, Alfred J. Wiley, brought his wife and two children to the station. His wife, Maralyn Joyce Wiley, who was 28, and the Wileys' two children, three-year-old Terry Lee, and one-year-old Rand Michael were on their way to visit Mrs. Wiley's mother, Mrs. Frank Collins of Burlington, Iowa. Mr. Wiley helped his family board car #1376. Before the train departed, Mr. Wiley left with his wife some magazines and gave his two young boys some chocolate. He then kissed his family good-bye and went to his job at the General Motors plant in LaGrange, Illinois. As Maralyn saw all the military personnel boarding the train, she couldn't help but think of her brother, Navy man Marvin Collins, who had been killed on August 9th, 1942 in the fighting off Guadacanal.

Private first class Raymond Jaeger, although only 21, was already married. In fact, at the time he and his wife Helen had four children. During his service time he had been wounded in the left arm by shrapnel while fighting in Okinawa. Bone from his right leg had to be grafted unto his arm to repair the injury. Jaeger had spent his convalescence in the Great Lakes Naval Hospital and was headed home on furlough to visit his wife and family. Pfc. Jaeger still had casts on his leg and arm. Since his home was in Burlington, Iowa, Pfc. Jaeger found a seat in the last car of the Advanced Flyer, NP 1376.

Mr. and Mrs. Henry Faber were also in that last car. A Marine who was discharged from military service just three days earlier, Faber had exited unscathed from some of the bloodiest battles in the Pacific fought over the past couple of years. He served as a litter bearer in the battle of Iwo Jima. Faber had arrived home in the states only last week. His wife met him at Great Lakes, Illinois and they were now traveling home to Keokuk, Iowa. While Henry had been serving his country overseas, his wife, Edith had been employed as a telephone operator at the local Bell exchange in Keokuk.

Sol Greenbaum, 27, also entered NP #1376 en route to his final travel destination that day - his home in St. Louis, Missouri. From his seat Sol could look out and see the Exposition Flyer pull out of Union Station alongside of and at the same time as the Advance Flyer. He then settled down and tried to shorten his trip by taking a nap.

Mrs. John Evjen of Carthage, Missouri was another passenger seated in the last car of the Advanced Flyer. Mrs. Evjen was the widow of former Carthage College professor, Dr. J.O. Evjen.

The widow had been visiting her son and daughter-in-law, Mr. and Mrs. Henry Evjen of Cleveland, Ohio. All three had then driven to Chicago to spend Easter with the two Evjen daughters, Miss Myrtle Evjen, a teacher at Elmhurst High School and Mrs. Douglas Hardy. After her visits to Cleveland and Chicago, Mrs. John Evjen was on her way back home to Carthage.

Twenty-eight-year-old Bernard "Barney" Voss, must have been an excited and anxious man as he entered car #1376. He had just received his honorable discharge from the Great Lakes Naval Station on Tuesday after serving his country for a little less than a year. He also was carrying a couple of gifts to give to his fiancée, Miss Bernice Klauser, when he would greet her back home in Quincy, Illinois. While in Chicago, Bernard had spent some time with his sister Rose, a Roman Catholic nun. He also had three brothers and another sister.

Al Miller was thirty-seven years old in 1946. He had been born in Remsen, Iowa and was the youngest of nine children. After the Miller farm was lost in the agricultural slump of the 1920's, his family moved to Chicago.

Al was an ambitious young man and after he earned his CPA he worked for a couple major Chicago firms before becoming self employed as an independent accountant. Miller met his future wife, Irene, at the Aragon Ballroom and the couple was married in 1939.

Al was also a partner in the Rivan Die Mold Tool and Die Shop in Villa Park, Illinois. Miller did the book work for his brother-in-law, Robert Rivan who ran the shop.

On April 25th, Al Miller was traveling to Canton, Missouri with John N. Ralston for a business meeting. Ralston was forty-six years old and a textile merchant for McCampbell Textile Company out of New York City.

Doctor and Mrs. Leo P. Moos were residents of Fargo, North Dakota. Leo was a dentist as was one of their sons, Lieutenant Theodore C. Moos who served in that capacity in the Army in Alameda, California. After a visit with Theodore's family, the Moos couple were now on their way to Galesburg, Illinois, to visit their other son, Lieutenant Colonel Daniel J. Moos. Daniel was a doctor on the staff of the Mayo General hospital in Galesburg.

Everett and Helen Conner were residents of South Bend, Indiana. Everett was thirty-five years old and had also recently been discharged from the Army. Conner had served with the 788th Ordinance company and had spent two years with this unit in both Italy and France. Since his discharge Conner had found employment with the Ford Hopkins Drug company. He was traveling to Hannibal, Missouri, by himself to surprise his father whom Everett had not seen since his discharge from the Army. Unfortunately, not being appraised of his son's intentions in advance, the father was not in Hannibal, but was in Kansas City visiting another son, Alvin. Actually, the elder Mr. Conner was leaving Kansas City on that same Thursday; but, headed not back to Hannibal, but to Albuquerque, New Mexico to visit his daughter. Everett's father was taking advantage of his sick leave from his work as a cutter with the International Shoe Company.

Another train traveler on her way to Hannibal was Mrs. Emma Bertha Schuetz of Lombard, Illinois. Emma, sixty-four years of age, was born in Germany and came with her parents to the United States in 1882 when she was three years old. In 1904 she married Louis Schuetz, whose life was tragically taken in 1933. Louis had been a special policeman and caretaker at the Lombard Village Hall. While he was attempting to stop a hold-up at a tavern located on Roosevelt Road near Rt. 53, south of Villa Park, Illinois, he was shot to death. The crime was never solved. Emma had continued to reside in Lombard, but since her husband's unsolved death, had been staying with her daughter, Edith Christianson and her family.

Emma had been planning a trip to Hannibal for the summer of 1946 to visit the family of another daughter, Mrs. Esther McClelland. However, since two of Esther's four children were sick, Schuetz decided to leave immediately so that she could be of help to the family.

In addition to Edith and Esther there were two more children in the Schuetz family, Mrs. Vierowena Smith of Indianapolis and Lewis H. Schuetz, also of Lombard.

Twenty-one-year-old Harry Long was another young soldier who had not long ago been discharged after a decorated career in the Army Air Corps. Harry had served as a waist gunner with the Seventh Service Command from September 13, 1943 to September 30, 1945. His plane had been shot down once over the North Atlantic and three times over Germany. These harrowing experiences earned for Long both an air medal and three oak leaf clusters. After his military service Harry went into the railway mail service and was today deadheading back to his home in Burlington, Iowa. Long was anxious to return home to his fiancée.

Hiram Stebbins' destination that day was Fort Madison, Iowa. Hiram would therefore be scheduled to sit in the last car #1376 along with all other passengers disembarking at Burlington, Iowa. When he entered the car, he noticed that the car was older and less comfortable than the rest of the units. He therefore went ahead and sat with a friend in a car closer to the front of the train – most probably the Silver Cloud. The conductor would shortly come to check Hiram's ticket and give a determination as to where he should be seated for the remainder of the trip.

Delbert Boon was a man in a hurry for the train to leave this Thursday. Boone was a sailor who was on a 72 hour leave from the Navy and anxious to visit his parents on the family farm in Clark county, Missouri, about 7 miles northeast of Luray, Missouri. Delbert was just 21 years of age, but was a first class Navy fireman who had already put in two years of service in the military. Although his parents would certainly be excited to see their son, it would be his June discharge from the Navy that they really were anticipating.

Seventy-three-year-old Joe Bentler must have been just a little tired boarding the train. A farmer, Bentler had transported livestock to Chicago on Wednesday and was now returning home to his farm between West Point and Houghton, near Fort Madison, Iowa However, Joe's schedule would not get any easier upon his return because Joe had eleven children, two of whom were in college and four of whom still lived at home. His wife, Diena (Holkamp) Bentler, had died nine years earlier in 1937.

Lucy Takashima's train ride from Chicago back to nursing school in Quincy, Illinois certainly was not the first bit of traveling she had done in her short 23 years. Lucy was born in Japan but came to the United States with her parents at a very early age. When the family first came to this country, they lived in California where Lucy graduated from high school. Her family then came to live in Chicago and in 1943 Takashima entered St. Mary's School of Nursing in Quincy. Lucy was boarding the Advance Flyer after spending her three week spring break with her father, sisters, and other relatives. Although she planned to graduate in June, her practicum would not be over until November.

First Lieutenant Kenneth Dickhut must have been on a natural high when he boarded the Advance Flyer. He was thirty years old, intelligent and ambitious. He was a graduate of the University of Illinois. Kenneth was a talented musician and twice on summer vacations during college he had traveled with orchestras to Europe. World War II was now over and Lt. Dickhut had four and a half years of service credit built up. Not long ago he had returned to the states from England. After a two week visit with his mother in Quincy, Illinois he traveled to Lewiston, Maine for a visit with his fiance, Irene Marcotte. Irene and Kenneth had met while both were stationed in San Diego, California two years ago. Marcotte was a lieutenant in the Army Nursing Corps. From Maine, Dickhut traveled to Chicago to visit his brother, Harold. Harold had encouraged his brother to extend his visit, but Kenneth was anxious to return to Quincy to study for the exam he needed to pass in order to become a certified public accountant.

While Lieutenant Dickhut had shortened a visit, another passenger, Mrs. Mary Langen had lengthened hers. The forty-nine year old Mrs. Langen had been in Chicago with relatives celebrating the Easter holiday. In all probability much talk was devoted to the twenty-fifth, silver wedding anniversary the Langens would be celebrating in just thirty-nine days on June 3rd. Instead of returning to Quincy with the other relatives, Mary stayed a few days longer to shop in the big city. Mr. C.S. Langen worked as a feed dealer and Mrs. Langen was very involved in a variety of religious and civic organizations in the community.

Another passenger, Mrs. Kay Lummis Flotkoetter, was also on the train that day because of a delay in plans. Kay Lummis had grown up in Quincy and had attended Quincy College. After she married Charles Flotkoetter, the couple moved to Chicago where Kay continued her education at Valparaiso University. On April 25, 1946, the twenty-two year old Mrs. Kay Lummis Flotkoetter, now living in Chicago, was traveling back to her former home in Quincy to attend the wedding of her brother-in-law. Her husband Charles had returned to Quincy on Wednesday, but Kay left a day later because she stayed and helped a friend take care of a newborn baby. Her brother-in-law, Robert Flotkoetter was scheduled to marry Roberta Busen on Saturday.

Nineteen year old Richard E. Howard, Navy Gunner's Mate 3rd class, had followed in his father's footsteps. His father, Leander Ray Howard was a World War I Navy veteran. Leander had been part of the "black gang", stoking coal engines aboard the U.S.S. Illinois as part of the Atlantic fleet. His ship was torpedoed and sunk with all hands on deck – all, that is, except Leander who was in the hospital with chicken pox!

Richard had just received his discharge from the Navy on Tuesday and was anxious to go home to Quincy and swap war stories with his Dad.

Clifford Yarbrough, who entered the last car, NP #1376, was also a Marine veteran. However, at fifty-eight years of age, Yarbrough's service to his country came in two earlier confrontations – the 1916 conflict with Mexico and World War I. In addition, he had been a civilian worker in the Pearl Harbor shipyards on December 7th, 1941. Although born and raised near Vandalia, Illinois, Clifford had recently been living in Quincy.

Among the many military personnel on the Advance Flyer were an Army – Navy combination sitting together. Private Elbert Hartman, a twenty-two-year-old soldier stationed at Fort Sheridan, Illinois (near Chicago) was on his way to spend a two week furlough with his mother in Stronghurst, Illinois. At the conclusion of his visit, Elbert was scheduled to report to a New Jersey Army post for duty overseas. Seated next to Hartman was Howard Stimpson, a sailor who had spent three years on the Pacific front. He survived his three year tour of duty without any injuries and received his discharge from the Navy that very morning! The two quickly found much to discuss.

Sixty-nine-year-old Mayme (Donovan) Mennen was boarding the Advance Flyer on the last leg of a series of visits to friends in Florida, Indianapolis, and Chicago. Mayme was born in DesMoines, but, early on, her parents moved to Burlington, Iowa. There she met and, at the age of thirty-eight, married P.L. Mennen in 1914. Mayme was quite an independent lady. She was involved in all sorts of community affairs including the Catholic Women's League where she served as president, the Daughters of Isabella, the Women's Auxiliary of Labor, Hawkeye Natives Society, Rosary Society of St. Patrick's, and the Women's Democratic Club.

Mayme's husband was the editor of the *Burlington Labor News* and also edited a weekly column for the *Hawk-eye Gazette*. The couple had an adopted son, John.

Ironically, there was another passenger boarding the train who had a connection with the *Hawk-eye Gazette*. Thirty-four-year-old Russell Whitehead was traveling with his wife, Eleanor, to Burlington, Iowa from Weymouth, Massachusetts. Russell had been employed as a printer in Boston for only a few months since his July 1945 discharge from the military. He had just accepted a job with the Burlington *Hawk-eye Gazette* as a linotype operator. Walter Sharp, the foreman of the *Hawk-eye Gazette* composing room was scheduled to meet the Whiteheads upon their arrival at the Burlington station at 3:42pm on April 25th.

Russell Whitehead was born in Dorchester, Texas on May 31, 1911. His parents (Charlie L. and Georgia B.) moved their family to Hereford, Texas when Russell was six years old. After graduating from Hereford High School in 1932, Russell worked as a printer for the *Hereford Brand,* the *Amarillo Daily News*, and finally the *Amarillo Times*. Russell then enlisted in the Navy on October 16th, 1941, in Dallas, Texas and was trained at the South Weymouth Naval Airbase in Massachusetts. He then served for over three years as a first petty officer whose rate was printer aboard the U.S.S. Lexington c-16. In fact, Whitehead was one of 2,600 officers and enlisted men who were on board the famous World War II aircraft carrier when it was first commissioned on February 17, 1943.

Eleanor Francis Burke was born in Pittsfield, Massachusetts, on April 11, 1911. Eleanor's parents were John and Winifred Burke. The Burke family originally lived in Boston but then moved to Weymouth when John found work as a moulder in a shipyard in the neighboring community of Quincy, Massachusetts. It was on the Fore River Shipyard in Quincy where the U.S.S. Lexington was built and it was likely that John helped build the ship on which his future son-in-law would serve! After high school, Eleanor found employment as a typist.

It was the combination of the above listed circumstances that brought Russell and Eleanor together. They were married and then Russell served aboard the Lexington for seven sail tours over most of the next three years.

After his discharge in July of 1945, Whitehead worked briefly once again for the *Hereford Brand* until he secured his short-lived job with the Boston paper. Perhaps the couple wanted a more neutral residence than the hometown of either spouse and thus took the opportunity that was presenting itself in Burlington, Iowa. The Whiteheads boarded the Advance Flyer en route to Russell's new employment with the *Hawk-eye Gazette* with renewed optimism.

☆ ★ ☆

Marine Sergeant Glenn Craft was stationed at Chicago's Great Lakes Naval Center. Sergeant and Mrs. Craft had just gotten married at the beginning of April, 1946. His twenty-three-year-old wife was the former Marian Joanna Brickman of Mendon, Illinois, a small town near Quincy, Illinois. The newlywed couple lived at 1742 Victoria Street in North Chicago. On Thursday morning, after Glenn left for the naval center, Marion was shocked when she received a telegram that her father was very seriously ill and that his death was imminent. Mrs. Craft packed quickly and and rushed to catch the noon train (Advance Flyer) to Quincy. From there, relatives would help her complete the journey to Mendon. Marion didn't have time to make verbal contact with her husband, but left him this note: "Dear Glenn – I think I can make the noon train. I will write you as soon as I can. Pay the rent. Watch the ice pan. - Marion". Boarding the train Marion was obviously in a somber mood and was hopeful that she might arrive in her hometown in time to say her final goodbyes to her father. Because of her destination, Marian entered the last car of the Advance Flyer, Northern Pacific car #1376.

Elves A. King, sixty-nine years old, was a former president of Bellevue (Ohio) Savings Bank. Prior to that experience his resume' included employment with the Ohio Cultivator Company from 1906 until 1920. Elves currently was a general sales manager for the New Haven, Connecticut, Trixy Corporation a maker of corsets, girdles, and brassieres. King was on the Advance Flyer with a ticket to Galesburg. From there he intended to travel to Bloomington, Illinois, for a business meeting.

The Hartford Insurance Company's chief investigator for the legal department of its fire insurance branch boarded the train that Thursday morning. Albert Lane was 56 years old. He and his wife Hazel had two children - a seventeen year old son, John A., and a nineteen year old daughter, Mary Claire.

A recent transplant from New Orleans to Chicago was thirty-five-year-old Edward Reed Sherwood. Highly educated and industrious, Sherwood was an honor graduate of Tulane University, '30, where he was the manager of the track team and a member of the Alpha Tau Omega fraternity. After graduation he worked for Consolidated Millinery until the beginning of World War II. He worked as a reserve officer in the Naval Supply Corps during the conflict and only recently received his discharge from the Navy. At that time he took up residence in Chicago.

He was married and Edward and his wife Catherine (Ernst) Sherwood had an eight-year-old son, Edward R. Sherwood Jr.

Mrs. Florence Whitehouse and her twenty year old daughter, Mrs. Irene Cook also entered the last car. The Whitehouse family was originally from England, but had moved to Schenectady, New York during World War II. After their marriage, George and Irene Cook also lived in Schenectady where George was employed as a draftsman for General Electric.

Then GE transferred Mr. Cook to a position in Kahoka, Missouri. George had traveled to Kahoka on Monday to look for an apartment. Florence Whitehouse offered to accompany her daughter when she took the train trip to join her husband.

Harry Whitehouse took his wife and daughter to the Schenectady train station. Prior to the train's departure a man named Roy Summers came up to Whitehouse and asked him if anyone from his party was traveling to Chicago.

Summers was the nephew of Mrs. Anne Hovey. Mrs. Hovey was seventy two years old and originally from Keokuk, Iowa. In 1943, after Anne's husband died, she decided to take her foster son, Carl, and move to Cohoes, New York to be near her nephew. After Carl enlisted in the Army, Mrs. Hovey decided to return to the more familiar surroundings of Keokuk.

When Roy Summers took his aunt to the train station, he was concerned about her ability to make the proper transfers, both in Chicago, and then again, in Burlington, Iowa. Since Florence and Irene's journey would take them through Keokuk, they readily agreed to accompany and take care of Anne during the entire course of the trip. During the trek from New York to Chicago, the three women shared experiences and enjoyed each other's company.

☆ ☆ ☆

Passengers on the Silver Inn, Silver Cloud, Silver Gleam

(11th, 10th, and 9th cars of the 13 car Advance Flyer)

Paratrooper Wesley "Blaine" Overman was born in 1925 in Beloit, Kansas. During the Dust Bowl of the '30's, his family moved to Caldwell, Idaho. Overman was seated in the fourth car from the end of the train, the Silver Cloud. Immediately behind his seat was a mother with a little baby in her arms. Blaine was sitting on the aisle next to a rather large man. Although he was hungry, Blaine early on decided not to eat in the train's diner. Instead, he was going to wait and build an appetite for one of those big steaks when he reached Omaha, Nebraska. From Omaha he would take the Portland Rose for the remainder of his trip home to visit his parents. Blaine was on a two week furlough from Camp Campbell, Kentucky.

Another man boarding the Silver Cloud was George Whitney from Council Bluffs, Iowa. Whitney was looking forward to returning home after four years in the Navy during the war.

Also entering the Silver Cloud was twenty year old Thomas Chaney, a steward in the Merchant Marines. Chaney was traveling cross country from New York to San Francisco, but along the way had scheduled a stop in Council Bluffs to visit his parents. Thomas also entered the Silver Cloud and sat next to another Council Bluff resident, Fred Robinson. Robinson was 62 years old and a respected Council Bluffs businessman. Originally from Ohio, Fred became owner of Chieftain Motor Sales in Council Bluffs in 1939. On the morning of the 25th he was returning from an automobile dealer's conference.

Shortly after the train left Chicago's Union Station, Chaney and Robinson decided to eat lunch in the dining car, the Silver Inn – the third car from the end of the Advanced Flyer.

Mr. and Mrs. John A. Sromovsky were also originally on the 4th car from the rear, the Silver Cloud, but moved back one car to eat in the Silver Inn diner car. Sophie Sromosvsky was twenty-nine years old and the couple had been married less than three months. After their marriage on January 28th Mrs. Sromovsky lived with her sister and brother-in-law, Mr. and Mrs. Vincent Sitkowski of Plymouth, Pennsylvania. In the meantime, Master Sergeant Sromovsky received his assignment to his new post at Fort Robertson, Nebraska. After traveling to the fort and locating housing he returned to Plymouth for his wife. The couple were traveling by train to their new post. Upon boarding the train, the couple found they were hungry, entered the third car from the rear of the train, the Silver Inn, and each ordered a bowl of soup.

The couple was looking forward to a long life together. This had not been the case for Sophie's grandparents. Sophie's grandfather had died in the Baltimore Tunnel disaster of June 5th, 1919, a tragedy that claimed 92 lives.

An elderly couple from Escanaba, Michigan, Mr. and Mrs. Matt Lawrence were traveling to visit their son, Matt Jr and his family in Ottumwa, Iowa. Mr. Lawrence was eighty years old and born in Oshkosh, Wisconsin. Mrs. Lawrence was 71 years old and born in Wales. The couple had spent the winter in Greenwich, Connecticut with their oldest son, Craig. They then traveled to Whitehall, New York to spend Easter with Mrs. Bessie Bascom, Mrs. Lawrence's sister. They were taking the Advance Flyer in order to visit their son Matt Jr. and his family. Mr. Lawrence had retired 10 years ago after a long career as a manager of the American Express Company in Escanaba.

August H. Anderson was certainly no stranger to the Burlington line. He had been working for the rail line for the past 43 years and for the last 17 years he was Burlington's chief scale inspector. Anderson is a very familiar Swedish name, and indeed, August was born in Sweden and brought by his parents to this country at the age of four. While his parents located in Tabor, Iowa, August, in seeking employment, eventually would settle in Lincoln, Nebraska (where the CB & Q's primary scales for weighing all railroad cars were located). There he met Helen Bersten and the two were married in 1905. The couple had two sons, Mark who lived in Portland, Oregon and Ralph who also lived in Lincoln. August was 68 years old.

Dorothy Lee (Lendrion) Aman grew up in Cleveland, Ohio and graduated from South High School. She lived with her mother, Julia. In 1943 Dorothy left home and joined the Marines. While stationed in Santa Barbara, she met her future husband, Marine Corporal William Aman. When William returned from his tour of duty in the Pacific, the couple married on September 15, 1945.

After the couple were discharged from the service, William found employment with the Watson Brothers Trucking Company in Omaha, Nebraska. In February the couple tried to drive back to Cleveland to visit Dorothy's mother and to give Julia the exciting news that she was to become a grandmother. Unfortunately, the Aman's car broke down about 50 miles outside of Omaha and the couple had to postpone their trip.

William could not take more time off so soon after his employment, so, Dorothy took the train by herself and stayed to visit with her mother for 10 days. Obviously Dorothy and her mother must have had a wonderful time discussing the exciting details and preparations needed for the baby's arrival in early fall. As Dorothy boarded the Advance Flyer, she must have been in a great frame of mind picturing future visits to Cleveland with her husband and baby.

Mrs. Florence Wilson was traveling alone this day. Florence, in her mid-forties, was the wife of Dr. Harold K. Wilson, head of the Department of Agronomy at Pennsylvania State College. The couple had no children. Dr. Wilson had been on the faculty at the University of Minnesota before being appointed to his present position. Florence and Harold had left State College on Wednesday and went along separate paths at that juncture. Dr. Wilson was returning to the University of Minnesota for a visit and an examination of an experiment station. His wife boarded the Advance Flyer for a visit with her family in Birmingham, Iowa.

Shortly after the train left the station, Florence entered the Silver Inn dining car for lunch.

Mary Farley was a 42 year old, single, career woman who was the manager of Lyon and Healy Company whose headquarters were in Chicago. Lyon and Healy had an interesting history of manufacturing musical instruments. Historically they are best known and respected for the production of harps. Mary's family was from Omaha, Nebraska which was her destination when entering the Silver Cloud.

Seventy-one-year-old Mrs. Charlotte Collins had retired in 1945 and was now boarding the Advance Flyer after enjoying one of retirement's main benefits – the ability to travel to visit her children and grandchildren. Charlotte was returning to her home in Hannibal, Missouri, after a visit with her daughter and son-in-law, Mr. and Mrs. C.N. Hultberg, of Highland Park, Illinois.

Collins' husband, George Herbert Collins, Hannibal's former assistant postmaster, had died on September 27, 1924. Within a year after her husband's death, Charlotte took the job as deputy clerk of the U.S. District Court in Hannibal – a position she would hold for twenty-one years.

Mrs. Collins had a second daughter, Mrs. Robert Jackson of Kansas City. Charlotte looked forward to making many more such visits to both Highland Park and Kansas City. This morning her son-in-law, C.N. Hultberg, brought her to Union Station.

Abraham Rohr was seventy-five years of age. He had finally retired two years earlier from employment as a clothing salesman at Mandel Brothers department store. Abraham's wife was Elizabeth (Glatter) Rohr. The couple were on their way today to visit one of their two daughters, Hannah, whom they called "Honey". Honey Riseman lived in Omaha, Nebraska with her husband Charles Riseman. The Rohr's other daughter was named Sadie.

Thirty-two year old Leona Belle Saylor, an excited traveler that day, had grown up in Brunswick, Nebraska, never married, and was now working for the government in Washington, D.C. Her vacation came earlier than she had expected and so now Saylor was planning a surprise visit to see her parents, Clayton and Gladys. The only local person who knew of her impending surprise was her friend, Mrs. Dorothy Miller Wilcox of Grand Island with whom Leona had planned to spend Thursday night before completing her final leg of her journey to surprise her parents.

Kenova, West Virginia resident, twenty-five year old Sergeant Elza Lett Jr., was discharged from the Army four months ago after a four year term of service in the South Pacific. Two weeks ago Elza left his home in West Virginia and traveled to New York. From there he sent word to his parents that he was traveling by train to Nebraska to accept employment. Elza has two sisters, Mary Lett and Mrs. John Clause and two brothers. His two brothers both opted for service in the Navy - Walter was stationed at St. Augustine, Florida and Richard Lee, was in Alameda, California.

STAFF ON THE DINING CAR, THE SILVER INN

The dining staff of the Advance Flyer were on the train before any of the passengers. The diner was called the Silver Inn and it was the third car from the end of the train. Meals would be available shortly after departure and the cooks, wait staff, and the dining car steward were making sure everything was in readiness for the lunch crowd.

The working staff of the dining car included cooks and waiters under the management of the dining car steward. The steward was a man from Berwyn, Illinois named Arthur "Ray" Abbott. Abbott, and his friend, Clyde DeMille, both WWI veterans had, after their military service, bought a tiny cigar store and newspaper stand. The two enlarged the store to include a soda fountain and sandwich menu. Ray eventually bought out Clyde and further enlarged the establishment to what became known as The Sweet Shop, a very popular local hangout for Morton High and Morton Junior College students.

The Sweet Shop had the makings of a good business; unfortunately the kind-hearted Ray Abbott didn't run a good business. Over the years many of his customers took advantage of his good nature and they had been allowed to run up huge tabs that ultimately bankrupted the enterprise. Abbott had to find another source of revenue and was hired as the dining car steward for the Burlington's Advance Flyer. His new job placed him aboard the Advance Flyer on April 25th, 1946.

The chief cook on the train was a man named Don Donegan. Donegan was the father of famous boogie woogie queen, Dorothy Donegan. His second cook was Lavelle E. Neal.

Daniel Carr, William McBride, Charles Chamberlain, Ralph Brown, and Charles W. Butler were all members of the dining car's wait staff.

Carr was single and had worked for the Burlington line for four years.

Chamberlain, at 45 years of age and highly educated (graduate of Alcorn College), was the most popular member of the dining car staff. Charles had a 25 year old daughter and a 21 year old son who was at the time serving as a member of the U.S. European Occupational Forces.

Ralph Brown was 47 years of age and had worked on second and odd shifts for the train line for two years. He had only very recently won out over another employee for the assignment on the Advance Flyer's regular run.

Both the engineer, Wallace "William" Blaine and the fireman for the Exposition Flyer, Curtis H. Crayton lived in Galesburg, Illinois.

In less than a week, Crayton would be celebrating his 46th birthday. He had served 24 years as an engineman on the Burlington line. Crayton was born in Trenton, Missouri and married Dorothy Horner on May 10th, 1919. The couple had lived in Galesburg, Illinois since he started working on the railroad. The Craytons had a son, Melvin R. Crayton and a daughter, Mrs. Patricia E. Friend. Curtis loved to hunt and fish, was a member of both the local Masonic Lodge and the Brotherhood of Locomotive Firemen and Engineers.

On April 23, 1943, Crayton's brother-in-law Fred E. Bishop died in a horrible train accident. Bishop was the engineer of the gas-electric train that collided with a freight locomotive in Aurora, Illinois. He died when flames trapped him in the cab of his train.

Today, Curtis was in the cab of the Exposition Flyer along with the train's engineer, W.W. Blaine. Nothing in the two men's history could have possibly prepared them for what was to happen just a half hour into their journey.

CHAPTER 4 - THE CRASH

Will the Lights Be White?

Oft, when I feel my engine swerve,
As o'er strange rails we fare,
I strain my eyes around the curve
For what awaits us there.
When swift and free she carries me
Through yards unknown at night,
I look along the line to see
That all the lamps are white.

The blue light marks the crippled car,
The green light signals slow;
The red light is a danger light,
The white light, "Let her go."
Again the open fields we roam,
And, when the night is fair,
I look up in the starry dome
And wonder what's up there.

For who can speak for those who dwell
Behind the curving sky?
No man has ever lived to tell
Just what it means to die.
Swift toward's life's terminal I trend,
The run seems short to-night;
God only knows what's at the end -
I hope the lamps are white.
                    –Cy Warman

The Exposition Flyer's run to Oakland, California lasted from 1939 to 1949. Over this time the two most devastating accidents affecting the Expo took place within a one month period of time in 1946.

On April 5, 1946, in Pilot, Nevada, the Exposition Flyer jumped the tracks because of excessive speed trying to navigate a siding switch at a construction site. The derailment killed two passengers and injured seven others.

Then, just 20 days later, on April 25th, 1946 came the Naperville rail tragedy...the greatest calamity in Burlington history.

By the end of the third week of April, 1946, the weather in Naperville was certainly teasing residents with the thought that perhaps they were in for an early summer season. On Easter Sunday temperatures reached 82 degrees and then rose another two degrees on Monday. The thermometer dropped slightly into the mid seventies on Tuesday and Wednesday.

Thursday, April 25th, was still pleasant with temperatures hovering in the high 60's accompanied by clear skies. Pictures of the day show a good number of the crowd with top coats and light jackets. The weekend after Easter would see a cold front continue to drop temperatures into the 50's.

The Exposition Flyer, i.e., train #39, would leave each day for San Francisco from Chicago's Union Station at 12:35pm. On another track, at the exact same time each day, the Advance Flyer, #11, would also depart from the station. Its destination was Burlington, Iowa, and then Omaha and Lincoln Nebraska.

At Kedzie Avenue, after traveling a distance of 4.83 miles, train #39 merged on to track #2, a short distance behind the Advance Flyer. From then on, the trains ran on the same track at speeds of 80 to 85 mph and while being separated by an interval of only two to three minutes.

As was mentioned in the last chapter, those passengers destined for Burlington and points south of Burlington were riding in the last car of the Advance Flyer. That car, #1376, was not a Burlington car, but was on loan from the Northern Pacific on a per diem mileage basis. Since the Northern Pacific Railroad owned 97% of CB & Q stock, this lending of a consist (i.e., car) from a "family" railroad was a common practice. The Advance Flyer was scheduled to arrive in Burlington at 3:42pm. At Burlington, Iowa, the 1376 would be taken off the Advance Flyer and its passengers transferred to the Mark Twain Zephyr. Car #1376 could not just be coupled unto the Mark Twain, because that Zephyr was an articulated train, meaning it was a train with each of the cars permanently connected to its adjacent car by a common set of trucks, i.e., wheels. The train was 280 feet long and its cars were joined with a sleeve joint; the purpose of that design was to eliminate slack action between cars. The Mark Twain was then scheduled to leave Burlington at 4 pm arriving into Quincy at 5:58pm.

After they left Union Station, the Advance Flyer, quickly followed by the Exposition Flyer, sped through the towns of Chicago suburbs of Cicero, Berwyn, Brookfield, La Grange, Western Springs, Hinsdale, Clarendon Hills, Westmont, Downers Grove, and Lisle. The Advance Flyer and the Exposition Flyer were due to pass through Downers Grove, a community 7 miles east of Naperville, at 12:56pm and 12:58pm respectively. According to information supplied at the time by Burlington officials, as it passed Downers Grove, the Exposition Flyer was approximately two minutes late and there was an interval of about three minutes between the two trains. Railroad authorities stated that an interval of three minutes would keep the two trains four miles apart.

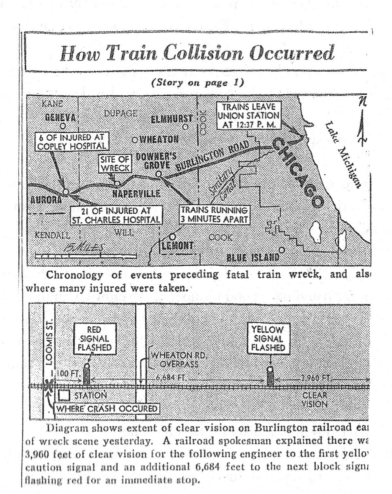

How Train Collision Occurred

(Story on page 1)

Chronology of events preceding fatal train wreck, and als where many injured were taken.

Diagram shows extent of clear vision on Burlington railroad ea of wreck scene yesterday. A railroad spokesman explained there wa 3,960 feet of clear vision for the following engineer to the first yello caution signal and an additional 6,684 feet to the next block sign flashing red for an immediate stop.

"Map from April 26, 1946 edition of the The Chicago Sun shows the path that the Advance Flyer and the Exposition Flyer followed from Union Station 28 miles southwest to the point of their crash just east of the Naperville train station. Despite the notation on the map, both trains left Union Station at 12:35pm.

Because of the speed of the two trains and their close proximity to each other, there were light signals to alert the trailing train of trouble ahead. If a proper distance between the two trains was maintained, a green (CLEAR) light would signal that everything was OK. If, however, the Exposition Flyer would narrow its distance from the Advance Flyer, a yellow (APPROACH) caution light would alert the engineer of the trailing train to back off a bit. According to the Burlington Historical Society Bulletin #44, "Burlington rules require that when a distant signal is displaying a restrictive indication, trains must reduce speed at once and move at 'restricted speed' until the indication of the next governing signal can be determined. Restricted speed means proceed prepared to stop short of train, obstruction, or anything that may require the speed of the train to be reduced." However, it was not uncommon for the engineer of the trail train to "play the yellow", or to push the envelope when it came to speed. This action would trigger a yellow light. Then all the engineer would have to do is to back off the train's speed just a little bit knowing that he'd be rewarded with a green light at the next light signal. Because of this cat and mouse game, it was rare for trains separated in this manner to have a green light for the majority of their journey. The other color option for a signal light of course was red (STOP IMMEDIATELY).

On April of 1946 there were three main rail tracks in Naperville, Illinois. On track numbers 1 & 2, trains moved in each direction (east to west or west to east). Track #3 (the southernmost of the three rails), was for eastbound trains only.

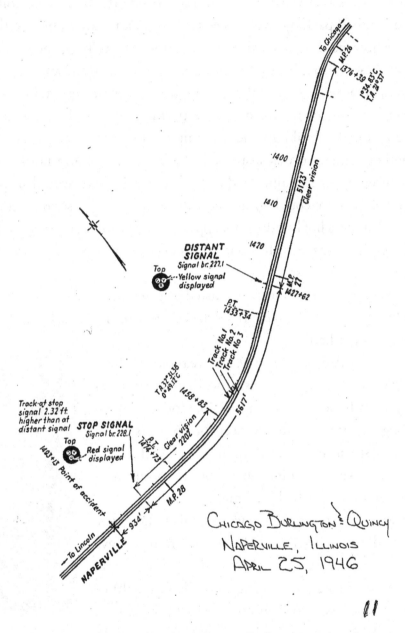

Diagram from ICC report (see appendix for full text of ICC report) that shows tracks, degree of curve, light standards, and point of impact at time of Naperville train wreck, April 25, 1946.

As it turns out, as the Advance Flyer was approaching Naperville, Sherman Grant, the brakeman riding in one of the last cars of the Advance Flyer, "saw an object with a silvery gleam come out from what looked like the car ahead." He thought that there might be a mechanical problem and so Grant notified Conductor John E. Aue who had the train stopped. The train slowed down just as it was rounding the bend and coming into Naperville. At 1:03pm the Advance Flyer stopped just 1,097 feet east of the Naperville station with the last twenty-five percent of the train blocking the Loomis Street intersection.

Usually, when a train made an unexpected stop the cause had to do with something called a "hotbox" problem. In 1946, a train's axle and bearings were generally housed in what was called a bearing box or journal box that was covered by a lid. Inside the box was an oil reservoir and oil-soaked rags or threads called packing that allowed oil to wick up and lubricate the bronze bearing. Before roller bearings became the standard, it was common to see brakemen walking with oil cans checking oil levels in these journal boxes. On occasion, when the train was stopped at night, hobos would take oil from these boxes to use for their camp fires. So, these journal boxes had to be checked often. If the oil level got low, or if threads of the packing got caught between the axle and the bearing, friction would quickly build up and the unit would overheat and produce what was called a "hotbox". If a "hotbox" situation was suspected, the brakeman would notify the conductor who would have the engineer stop the train. At that time the brakeman would inspect the boxes and correct the situation before a fire could ignite and cause a much more serious set of problems.

However, in this instance, a hot box does not appear to be the direct motivation for the conductor's action to stop the train. In retrospect, the conductor's decision to stop the train after the Naperville curve was regrettable to say the least.

The bottom line is that the situation now existed that featured a stopped advance train, hidden by a curve, followed by a train on the same track, less than three minutes behind, traveling at speeds between 80 and 85 miles per hour.

The engineer aboard the Advance Flyer was 68 year old, Wallace "William" Blaine from Galesburg, Illinois. The Exposition Flyer engineer was a 44 year railroad veteran and eligible for retirement in two years. Although Blaine was an engineer for 36 years, most of this time had been spent as a "yard engineer" in Galesburg, Illinois. His seniority, however qualified him for the position as "road engineer", an assignment he had held more recently.

When the Advance Flyer stopped, two signal lights were automatically triggered some distance behind the train to give warning to the Exposition Flyer. First, there was a yellow signal (227.1) operating some 6,551 feet (according to the ICC graph) or 6,851 feet (according to the ICC text) behind car #1376, the last car of the now stationary Advance Flyer. Light signal 227.1 was 7,648 feet east of the Naperville Train Station. 5,617 feet west of that first yellow light signal (227.1) was a second signal (228.1) which was now illuminated "red" in order to warn the fast approaching

Exposition Flyer engineer William Blaine. Picture from Life Magazine May 20, 1946, p30G.

Exposition Flyer to stop. 934 feet west of signal 228.1 would be the point of the collision in this tragedy. Finally, the point of collision was 1,097 feet east of the Naperville Train Station.

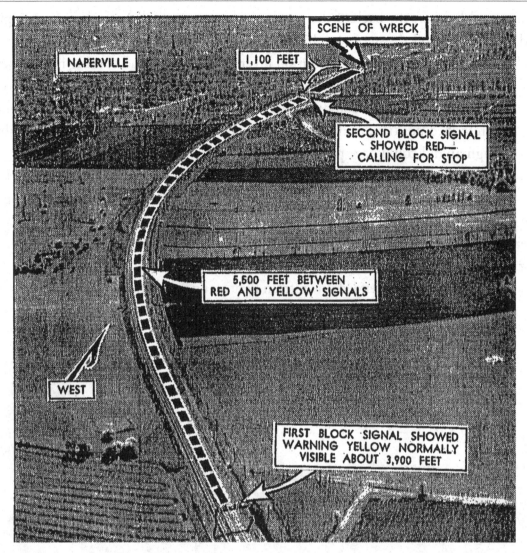

Markings on photo from Chicago Tribune archives indicate the path of the Exposition Flyer and the vision problems the engineer encountered as he approached the Naperville curve.

It should be remembered that the Advance Flyer was around the bend and out of sight of the fast approaching Exposition Flyer. Also, as mentioned above, it was not unusual for a yellow light to be seen by the follow-up train. Blaine's first reaction was probably to slow down a bit rather than to apply the brakes.

There was still another unfortunate circumstance associated with the stop of the Advance Flyer. Usually, in case of just such a stop, it would be the job of the flagman on the advance train to drop warning fuses (ie., flares) upon the track, switch on the oscillating red light on the rear car, and then to flag down any approaching following train.

The flagman for the Advance Flyer, James Tangney, later admitted that he was not in his prescribed position in the last consist, car #1376, when the conductor signaled for the train to stop. Instead, he was in the second last car, the Mississippi. Tangney had to run from the Mississippi and then through car#1376 before he could pick up his flag equipment, exit the train, and move up the tracks in an attempt to flag down the quickly approaching Exposition Flyer. Since he was not in the back of the train, he was unable to drop fuses as the train slowed; nor did he have time to switch on the oscillating red light on the back of the coach. As he ran through both the Mississippi and car #1376 and then jumped off the steps with his flag, he yelled back "I'm going to try to stop that train behind us." As Engineer Blaine of the Exposition Flyer rounded the bend coming into Naperville, he later reported: "Then I saw the train stalled ahead. Then I saw the flagman. He was only four or five car lengths behind the train. They couldn't have been stopped long." Even though Tangney could not get in his prescribed position, under the existing set of conditions, it seems very doubtful that anything the flagman did could have prevented what was about to happen.

In the engine cab of the Exposition Flyer, Engineer William Blaine and Fireman Curtis H. Crayton were probably not really convinced of any emergency situation until they rounded the bend. They must have been startled to see the red STOP signal that then appeared a bit beyond the Columbia Road Overpass. In 1946 the wooden bridge that spanned the tracks was higher arched than today's modern bridge. At the time, therefore, the engineer and fireman would have been looking under the bridge to see the red light that extended down from light standard number 228.1. They may very well have seen both the stopped train and flagman Tangney at the same time that they saw the red light.

April 27th, 1946 Chicago Daily News photograph east of crash site shows light signal 228.1 with block signals suspended below the cross beam and over tracks 1 and 2. Track #3 was reserved for eastbound trains. This set-up shows that Engineer Blaine had to look under the Columbia Street Bridge in order to see the block signal (red) and subsequently the stalled Advance Flyer. The advantage of time and study allowed the ICC to more accurately report that signal 228.1 was 934 feet from the crash site. Photograph from author's collection.

It was at that time that Blaine threw on the train's brakes, and sounded the horn. Both the engineer and the fireman on the Exposition Flyer had only seconds to decide if their chances of survival were greater if they jumped or if they stayed with the train. Crayton yelled to Blaine that "Looks like we're going into her Bill!" But the engineer was too focused to notice Crayton climb out of the cab and jump from the train.

Knowing at that point that a collision was inevitable, the engineer decided to stay in the cab of his train.

The Kroehler Furniture Manufacturing Company was located just to the north of where the Advance Flyer was stopped. The switchboard operator at the Kroehler Furniture Manufacturing Factory, Lillian Ory, had just come back from her lunch break.

The foreman of the lumber yard for Kroehler was thirty-five-year-old Harold Schrader who lived at 540 South Webster Street. Harold's job was to receive the lumber brought in by the trains, accept it, and store it in the Kroehler warehouse. Workers would then season the lumber in the kilns so that the wood could be used to make the framing for the upholstered furniture for which the company was so famous. Over the years, Harold had become programmed to expect the early afternoon passing by of both the Advance Flyer and the Exposition Flyer. On that fateful Thursday he saw the Advance Flyer stop unexpectedly and watched as the flagman and several other train employees got off the train. As he started to walk over to question these train officials, he saw the Exposition Flyer round the bend at a high speed and come down the track toward the stopped train. Schrader yelled at the train employees, "Get the hell out of there!", to warn them. He then turned to run into the office to have the switchboard operator initiate calls for rescue units to come to what he knew would be an impending emergency scene. As he was pivoting around, he noticed someone (Crayton) jump from the engine of the Exposition Flyer.

Rosie Hodel, was 21 years old at the time and lived with her family at 135 North Loomis Street, about 100 yards south of where the Advance Flyer had stopped. She had been temporarily laid off from her job at Kroehler and was at the time bartending at night to earn some money.

On that early afternoon Rosie Hodel was hanging clothes on the line. At the time, the Hodel residence was the first house on the west side of Loomis street after the railroad crossing, so Rosie had an unobstructed view of the train tracks. She too was familiar with the daily passing of the two express trains and took notice when the Advance Flyer stopped. The war had ended less than a year ago, and Rosie especially looked for, then waved to, the military personnel she saw sitting by some of the windows of the last car #1376. She was about ready to return to hanging clothes, when she saw the Exposition rounding the Naperville bend and closing in on the Advance Flyer. Hodel estimated that the speed of the second train moments before impact was approximately 50 to 55 miles per hour. Rosie "saw someone (Crayton) hanging from the ladder on the left hand doorway into the cab of the Exposition Flyer".

Living even closer to the train tracks than Rosie Hodel was Mrs. Anna Koppa-Miller. Anna lived with her husband Arthur at 406 E. Fourth Street, on the corner of Loomis Street and 4th Avenue. Anna had just started to wash the lunch dishes and was actually looking out the window when she noticed the Advance Flyer make an unexpected stop. Anna's house was only 75 feet from the train tracks and when she saw the first train stop, she went to her back door to wave with her kitchen towel at the soldiers aboard car #1376. When she arrived at the door she had an excellent view of the Exposition Flyer coming "lickety split" around the bend. She heard the brakes screech "terribly".

Inside car #1376, the last car of the Advance Flyer, passengers were confused as to the reason their train had stopped. Then one passenger from that car, Private First Class Raymond Jaeger, a twenty-one-year-old Marine stood up and went to the back of the car for a drink of water.

Jaeger had survived the fighting at Okinawa, but during that conflict he was injured in the arm by shrapnel. The Marine had a bone graft from his right leg to help fix the splintered bone in his left arm. Jaeger had spent weeks recuperating at the Great Lakes Naval Hospital and was now on the Advance Flyer anxious to return to his wife and four kids in Burlington, Iowa. Both his arm and leg were still heavily bandaged.

That decision to get up and quench his thirst probably saved Raymond's life. On the way to the rear of the car, he once again made a fuss over a baby that a young mother had in her arms. As he got to the back by the rear platform, he was startled and terrified to see the Exposition Flyer rapidly closely in on his train! "It came fast. I watched horrified. The train came on bigger and bigger. I saw a man (Curtis H. Crayton) climbing down from the engine cab, and start down the ladder. That's all I saw. I turned around and ran yelling warnings toward the front of my coach. The next second it hit".

Naperville resident, Larry Cena, had just turned 24 years old on March 19th. He had recently been discharged from military service and was now attending North Central College on the G.I. Bill.

As was his custom on Thursday, at a little before one o'clock, Cena was walking to the college campus to attend his psychology class. Since he lived at 711 Brainard Street, in order to get to his college class, he had to go across (north to south) the railroad tracks at the Loomis Street crossing.

This particular day the Advance Flyer had just made an unexpected stop and was blocking his path. Larry noticed the brakeman who was inspecting the undercarriage on the dining car.

Cena walked up to within 30 feet of the car and he could see into the Silver Inn and remembers seeing diners enjoying their meal. It was only "a few minutes, probably one or two minutes" before Cena "heard, felt, and witnessed a terrible collision which turned out to be caused by another passenger train."

Eye witnesses Cena, Shrader, Koppa-Miller, and Hodel did not want to believe the inevitable consequence of what was unfolding before them. The squealing of the Expo's brakes and the blaring of its horn ended in a thunderous crash. At 1:05pm E.S.T. the unstoppable force (Exposition Flyer) met the immovable object (Advance Flyer). The bullet nosed engine of the Expo rammed into and imbedded itself into car #1376 of the Advance Flyer. The engine's trucks (wheels) sheared off and rolled 18 feet to the west. The collision bent down the center sill of that last car a full 18 inches. That action allowed the engine to rise up, hover, thud down, and plow along the floor of that Northern Pacific car. The engine came to rest 3/4ths of the way through the last car which had been pushed 205 feet west of the original point of impact. The back car of the Advance Flyer was split wide open on the north side and the roof peeled open like a sardine can. Smoke and floating debris from the insulation from the cars enveloped the scene. After the crash there was a momentary silence before moans and screams started to emanate from the stricken cars of the Advance Flyer. All the deaths on train #11 ultimately were to occur in either the last car (thirteenth car) where passengers were crushed to death between the seats or in the lightweight eleventh car, the Silver Inn dining car. The Silver Inn was turned around and just about totally destroyed except for the kitchen area that was slightly more protected with metal framing.

Curtis H. Crayton would be the only fatality from the Exposition Flyer! Crayton's decision to jump from the cab could have been triggered subconsciously by the fact that only three years before, his brother-in-law died in a train wreck after being trapped by flames in his engine cab. Crayton was forty-five years old and was a Burlington engine man for twenty-four years. In just fifteen days Curtis and his wife, Dorothy Horner Crayton would have celebrated their 27th wedding anniversary. Curtis left behind his wife and two children, Melvin and Patricia. As it turned out, Crayton's fate was sealed no matter what action he would have taken. Pictures later showed that a large, jagged piece of the roof from the last car of the Advance Flyer pierced the window of the cab where Crayton normally would be situated. It most probably would have have impaled Curtis had he remained with Blaine in the engine cab of the Exposition Flyer.

Fireman Crayton's fate may have been sealed even if he had stayed in the cab during the crash. Picture shows a ragged piece of roof from the Advance Flyer that entered the cab exactly where Crayton would have been positioned. Photograph courtesy of Paul Hinterlong.

In retrospect engineer Blaine's survival was probably due to the fact that the Burlington engines had changed cab designs from shovelnoses to bullet noses where the cab was more recessed from the front of the train. After the crash, Blaine said he "made certain that all the diesel motors were shut down to avoid the possibility of fire." Because of the trauma of the impact, the accuracy of the engineer's recollection of the events immediately after the collision might have been affected. At the time, Arnie Hodel, Rosie's brother, was working for Knoche Construction Company and was helping to build a two story addition to the Kroehler Office complex. Arnie also had spent the last two years as a member of the Naperville Fire Department. Years later, Hodel would reflect on the events of the day:

> *"We heard the crash and realized what had (happened) because we heard the diesel blowing its horn just prior to the crash. As we ran toward the wreck the insulation from the cars was drifting all around. Our construction foreman who was familiar with diesel engines was the one that shut the engine of Exposition Flyer off."*

As with the history of most events, the passage of time often places additional interpretations that cloud the issue of what actually may have originally transpired.

Railroad buff Bill Barber once worked at the Electro-Motive plant that manufactured the Exposition Flyer's E-5s. Bill came to know "several employees that were sent out to the wreck to assist wherever possible. When they arrived at the wreck site, the engines were still idling on the Exposition Flyer's E-5s. They shut them down."

Volunteer fire fighter Arnie Hodel (wearing helmet #1) was a rescue worker at the crash site. Hodel later would become fire chief from 1965-1984. Arnie's sister Rosie was an eyewitness to the tragic event. Photograph courtesy of Paul Hinterlong.

Blaine crawled out of the cab and found his way to Mrs. Anna Koppa-Miller's house which was located just about 25 yards south of the tracks. There a doctor bandaged his blackened face and Anna gave him some coffee. He then stood outside and gazed at the destruction spread across the tracks.

Ex Burlington employee Jim Christen, a rail history buff dedicated to the research of the Naperville train wreck, reports the next very unusual set of circumstances. "Immediately following the crash, huge crowds gathered at the scene. Among them was Aurora resident Hopkins Peffers who, upon seeing fire and ambulance vehicles racing east through Aurora and learning of the incident, returned home, picked up his wife, and drove east to Naperville. Standing off to the side of the accident, Peffers soon found himself beside a tall man dressed in overalls and Kromer cap – obviously a railroader – who engaged him in conversation and remarked that he had to find a way to Aurora to catch a train. Mr. Peffers offered the man a ride, and a short while later, the three got into Peffers' car, left the scene of the crash, and drove off toward Aurora. En route, further conversation revealed that the man was No. 39's engineer – W.W. Blaine – who the stunned Peffers' dropped off at the CB&Q's Aurora depot." Apparently, someone at the depot recognized Blaine and realized that his condition called for further medical analysis and treatment and got him admitted to St. Charles Hospital.

☆ ☆ ☆

G.W. Hill was the conductor aboard the Exposition Flyer. At the time of the crash Hill had collected 38 tickets. After the crash Conductor Hill was the first person to attend to fireman C.A. Crayton who had bailed out of the engine cab immediately prior to the crash. Hill found that blood was gushing out of Crayton's mouth. The conductor reported that the fireman died a short time later.

Conductor Hill then surveyed the scene and noted "I don't know why in the world the whole mess didn't catch on fire. Diesel oil, which is highly inflammable, was pouring out of our engine tank and was over our shoe tops in some places. Folks were standing around in it smoking cigarettes." Hill's concern certainly was justified. The Exposition Flyer's diesel engines (9910A and 9910B) each carried 1200 gallons of fuel oil and 330 gallons of lubricating oil. The fuel could have been ignited not only from the cigarettes smoked by bystanders but also from the sparks from the acetylene torch used to try to free passengers from the wreckage. And, being in the first half hour of its trip, the Exposition Flyer was still at near full fuel capacity.

At the time of the wreck, Harold Schrader's nephew, Delbert Schrader was working as a contractor on a house near the corner of Fourth and Loomis Streets. He was among the first responders and helped build the scaffolding that was used to help extracate passengers from the train. When workers brought an acetylene torch that was used to start opening up the sides of the train, Delbert warned that there was too much oil spilled to safely work so close to the ground. So, the workers climbed to the top of the cars with their torch.

Thankfully, Private Raymond Jaeger passed out from the crash. When he regained conscientiousness, he saw a Marine nurse who had come to assist at the crash site. Jaeger called out to her, "Hey Marine, how about helping a fellow Marine!"

The nurse was 20-year-old Calista Wehrli, a member of the Marine Corps Women's Reserve. Calista was born and raised in Naperville and was at the time on leave from her assignment in Parris Island, South Carolina. "Calis" had come back to Naperville for her sister Marge's Saturday wedding. She had arrived home on Wednesday and was that morning leisurely catching up with local news at the family's house at 145 North Center Street. With most of the thirteen Wehrli kids at school, Calis, her mother Gert, and her sister Marge were having coffee and hemming dresses for the wedding.

The three women were startled by a loud crash and Calista's afternoon plans were about to suddenly change. She jumped up and quickly moved outside where she saw from her house part of a train raised in the air.

Calis and Marge, both trained in first aid, ran to the site. At first Calista was helping people out of the third and fourth cars (Silver Inn and Silver Cloud) from the rear of train #11. Then Assistant Police Chief Jack Meluck yelled to Calista to help him with the dead and injured in car #1376. Meluch was also a Latin and science teacher at the high school. Jack knew Calis very well because during the summer months the two managed the life guards at the Naperville Centennial Beach. At the time of the crash Meluch was teaching 8th grade general science in a classroom on the second floor on the east side of the high school. Years after the crash one of his students at the time, Jim Dudley, recalled that he had "never heard anything like it before or since to compare to it. ....One teacher thought it might be a boiler explosion at Kroehler". Shortly after the sound of the explosion from the area of Kroehler and the train tracks, the students could hear the sirens from the fire station. With that, Meluch ran out of the building, waited for the fire trucks to come by, hopped on board, and was very quickly at the crash site.

When Calista Wehrli crawled through a window of that last car, she saw Private Raymond Jaeger who called out to her for help. Raymond immediately asked Wehrli about the condition of the young mother and her very young child whom he had met earlier. Calista had to tell him that the mother was decapitated and the child had been crushed. Most likely the mother was Mrs. Maralyn Wiley and the child was her year old son Randy. Randy and his three-year-old brother Terry were the only children listed as fatalities. At that point, Private Jaeger broke down in tears. Miraculously, Jaeger was one of the few from the last car to come out of the wreck relatively unscathed. Calista rewrapped the Marine's leg cast which had separated at the knee.

Calista and Marge worked at the crash site for hours. After a few hours Marge was feeling sick and had to go home. Calista stayed until after dark, having worked for about eight hours assisting with the medical needs of the injured and helping to remove the dead from the train. She finally gave in when someone handed her two severed legs from the last car. She handed them back and made her way home.

Working at the crash site also left an indelible impression on Kroehler worker Ralph Landorf. Years after the crash Landorf related that he couldn't continue in his rescue efforts after he "came upon this woman holding her baby with her head cut off..."

*One of the few survivors from the last car of the Advance Flyer, Marine Raymond
Jaeger Jr. is being carried to an ambulance that will transport him to St. Charles
Hospital in nearby Aurora. Photograph from author's collection.*

The effect of the collision can clearly be shown in the scattered placement of the last five cars of the Advance Flyer. Car on lower left is derailed Silver Gleam, the fifth car from the end of the train. The relatively untouched heavyweight second last car, the Mississippi, and the prone Silver Cloud (fourth last car) frame the devastated Silver Inn diner (third last car). At the Loomis Street crossing the Expo has driven three-fourths of the way into the last car, #1376. Kroehler workers can be seen on the roof of the building normally used to dry lumber. Photograph courtesy of Paul Hinterlong.

Most eye witnesses both on and off the trains estimated that the Exposition Flyer plowed into the back of the Advance Flyer at a speed of approximately 50 to 55 miles per hour. The Interstate Commerce Commission's investigative report estimated the speed of the Expo was "not less than 45 miles per hour".

The destruction impressed the crowd who later observed the damage. Eye witness to the scene, Harold Schrader, later reflected that the collision "looked like a motor boat hitting the water with the spray flying". Mrs. Grubb who had been aboard the Expositon Flyer stated that the rear car of

No. 11 was "split open like a pea-pod". A first responder, Calista Wehrli, observed "that last train was peeled like a banana". High school student Jeanne Clemens (Aeby) thought the last car was "peeled back like an opened sardine can". The *Keokuk Daily Gate* reported that the last car "crumpled like the wood of a cigar box". The *Vandalia Union* newspaper reported that the "observation coach ... was literally sheared apart".

View from northeast....The Exposition Flyer has split open and plowed three-fourths of the way into the last car #1376 of the Advance Flyer. Photograph courtesy of Paul Hinterlong.

View from south of tracks. Rail cars from left to right – Silver Cloud (on its side), rubble left from Silver Inn dining car, and car #1376. Exposition Flyer can be seen inside car #1376. Rescue workers use acetylene torch to attempt to free trapped passengers. Notice Kroehler employees watching scene from roof and out windows. Bill Seiser photograph courtesy of North Central College Archives.

After the Exposition Flyer had torpedoed into the back of the Advance Flyer, assistance was called for immediately and arrived quickly. The neighboring Kroehler Furniture Company was dismissed for the rest of the afternoon and many of the 800 employees brought ladders and built scaffolding to assist in extricating bodies from the wreckage. There were many acts of individual heroism displayed by both the passengers themselves and by those who quickly came to the scene. Fortunately, a staffing being held at Aurora's St. Charles Hospital provided for a complete compliment of medical staff at the hospital, which was where the vast majority of the injured were taken. The resources and facilities of Aurora's Copley Hospital were also utilized. In addition Jim Carrahan and Connie Gross of the Chicago Chapter of the American Red Cross were just a few blocks away at the time giving first aid instruction to North Central College students. As a consequence they were quickly able to redirect their efforts and those of their students.

Kroehler nurse, Lenore Clow, would years later, as Mrs Sterling McDonald, reflect on the aftermath of the crash: "All of a sudden they started bringing bodies in. They laid the dead on the floor of the shipping room and covered them with tablecloths someone got off the (train) diner. …I bandaged cuts and splints for I don't know how long." (David Young, Chicago Tribune, May 1, 1988).

Rescue efforts could be facilitated only if there was adequate on-site communications in place. Dean Houston later reported that he was part of a task force to achieve this goal:

...'I was a groundman in the Q telegraph department on a job site in East Aurora. After lunch, the Division Lineman came by and said we were needed in Naperville due to the wreck. We installed drop lines and trackside telephones for use by the recovery teams to request equipment and supplies. After that, we pitched in wherever manual effort was needed, mostly to clear the tracks of all the scattered debris."

After the crash Rosie Hodel moved closer to the sight and when the insulation, debris, and dust settled, she was startled to see the faces of two small children smashed against one of the windows. They were probably the faces of three-year-old Terry and one-year-old Randy Wiley. She ran back to her house to put in a call to help, but by this time several calls had already been received and help was on its way.

Rosie returned to help at the crash site. After a while she went back to her house for some water. "When I tried to get back to my house, the Navy wouldn't let me in. I told them I lived there, but they wanted to see some identification. Of course, it was all in the house. I didn't argue with them. I just walked around the back and crawled through a window."

Rescue workers (left) remove bodies from the rubble of the Silver Inn. One of the victims is lying in foreground. Bill Seiser photograph courtesy of North Central College Archives.

49

Mrs. Koppa-Miller's future son-in-law, twenty-five year old military veteran Royal Lauing, was at the time working for his uncle at the Burgess Garage at the corner of Washington Street and Chicago Avenue, a stone's throw from Beidelman Funeral Home. At the sound of the crash Lauing stopped his work, and hurried with a friend to the crash site.

> *"I went along with him to do whatever needed to be done. When we got there we took two guys to the hospital in Aurora and they started arguing over who was hurt worse. I thought at least that was a good sign, because they were both hurt pretty bad and yet they managed to laugh about it."*

Lauing years later would clearly remember the sight of bodies lining the driveway of the funeral home as he walked past Beidelman's that evening. The bodies were waiting to be identified and were wrapped in the plain white paper that Kroehler factory used to wrap furniture.

C.N. "Spike" Flanders also has a clear recollection of the train wreck and its aftermath:

> *"I had been sent to my room for some sort of misbehavior. We lived at 49 South Mill Street. I remember hearing the trains hit. I yelled down the stairs to my mother 'that it was going to rain. I just heard thunder'. I got up and came down stairs and then began to hear sirens. I remember the bodies from the train wreck being delivered to the funeral home across the street from us. They were laid out on the grass behind the funeral home. They were covered with sheets. I remember peeking under the sheets until I was chased home...."*

After the collision, Larry Cena - North Central College student, ex G.I., and eye witness to the crash - saw several ("perhaps five or six") bodies that had been thrown by the accident from the impacted lead train. All of the bodies appeared dead except for a woman who had a very serious leg injury. Almost immediately people came to the scene to give assistance. Years later, Larry Cena would recall one man in particular whose name he remembered as "John". This man went up to Larry, who was on the north side of the tracks, and persuaded Cena to help him take the injured woman to get emergency treatment. John went and got a vehicle from the Kroehler auto fleet and the two men struggled, but managed to get the lady into the sedan. Since there was no hospital in Naperville at the time, John decided that they should take the woman to the Naperville Tuberculosis Sanitarium. The workers at the sanitarium reluctantly accepted the responsibility of caring for the lady and Larry and John returned to Naperville. By that time, the roads into town were clogged with emergency vehicles and curiosity seekers and the two men eventually had to abandon their car outside of town and walk home.

The May 2, 1946 edition of the *Naperville Sun* reported that on the day of the crash Dr. Clayton S. Whitehead, Naperville physician and surgeon employed at Aurora's Copley Hospital helped save the life of one of the injured passengers. Dr. Whitehead stated in the article that "Mrs. Florence Whitehouse of Cohoes, New York, was suffering from a badly mangled right leg, and had lost a great deal of blood. Dr. Moran of the sanatorium agreed with me that she would not live unless she was immediately hospitalized. We rode in the ambulance with her to Copley hospital, administering stimulants all the way to keep her alive. The patient was taken into surgery about 9 o'clock Thursday night at which time her leg was amputated just above the knee. A broken bone punctured through the flesh of her left leg. A section of the bone had to be removed, but the leg is now in a splint with a good prospect of saving it."

Ethel Widder was hanging clothes in the back yard of her brother-in-law's house at 252 Fourth Avenue, a home directly across the street from where the Advance Flyer had stopped unexpectedly. Ethel's husband, John (whom everyone called "Bud") had recently returned from military service. The couple were staying with Bud's brother's family until they could afford a place of their own. Bud, and his brother, Art, were at a painting job at the time of the crash. Art's wife, Florence, had taken her two children to visit her sister.

Ethel was home alone with her baby daughter, Carole Ann. Carole Ann was in the playpen while her mother hung the clothes to dry.

Mrs. Widder remembers the sound of the collision as being "a very monstrous thud". When word spread of the collision, Bud and Art left their painting job and morphed into their responsibilities as volunteer firemen and hurried to the scene.

At some point, Ethel remembers, Rosie Hodel brought over a small baby and asked if Ethel would watch over it while someone was attending to its mother's injuries. Rosie couldn't take care of the baby herself because she was helping at the scene.

Harold Huth lived at the foot of the Columbia Street Bridge that passed over the tracks just around the bend coming into Naperville. Huth was a truck driver for Kroehler and was having his cab checked at the Kroehler garage in the very early afternoon of April 25th. He too noticed the unusual stop of the Advance Flyer and walked over for a closer look. When he was only about 20 feet from the tracks he heard the loud, constant whistle of the Exposition Flyer accompanied by sparks coming out from all the train's wheels. Then a train employee in a white jacket jumped off the Silver Inn dining car and ran past him up Loomis Street. That waiter was probably S.A. Davcis, who later testified that he got out with conductor Aue when the train stopped. Davcis later affirmed that he ran in anticipation of the impending disaster. Davcis' attention had certainly been focused to the approaching train by Kroehler yard foreman, Harold Schrader, who had shouted "Get the hell out of there!" At that point, Huth says that he also turned and started running and actually passed the train employee!

Dick Rechenmacher, had recently returned from the service in the Coast Guard and was working on a car at his home just a block from the Loomis Street train track intersection. Dick was among the first to come upon the scene and worked long and hard in assisting those in need. At the end of the day, Naperville fire chief Charles Foucek as well as assistant fire chief, Jack Meluch, suggested that the young, recently discharged sailor would make an excellent fire fighter. Rechenmacher later attributed his experience at the train wreck and those words of encouragement as the incentives to start a long career as a Naperville fireman. Dick was my wonderful uncle. Two of Dick's sons would eventually follow in their father's footsteps as firefighters. My uncle Dick, along with two other Naperville firefighters, was to die tragically on December 7, 1970 when his fire truck was hit by a semi-trailor truck as the firecrew was responding to a fire west of the city.

Dick's sister, my aunt Helen Rechenmacher, was a secretary at Kroehler. She had just turned nineteen years old on April 10th. Because she was the ninth of twelve children she had been anxious to get a part time job while still in high school in order to help out her family and to begin a career. Her family lived on Loomis Street just a block from Kroehler and the Loomis Street train intersection. Her high school, Naperville High School (converted to Washington Jr. High in 1950), was less than three blocks west of the Kroehler factory. During her senior year Helen had noticed a help wanted ad from Kroehler on the high school bulletin board. It proved to be the perfect job opportunity for Helen. She applied for and got the job as typist for the factory's production department. The school allowed Helen to drop last period band in order to meet the hours required for the job. Her first job at Kroehler was typing labels for furniture. She worked five days a week from two to five each afternoon. After just a short while, Helen was promoted and her next job included receiving and sending telegrams. That ability would be in demand on the afternoon of April 25th.

In the office where Helen worked, surprisingly, no one heard the sound made by the train wreck. Her boss informed her of the accident and Helen was soon put to use sending telegrams for people who survived the wreck. She sent quite a few of these messages and then volunteered in the kitchen making sandwiches. The cafeteria staff and volunteers served sandwiches and beverages.

According to The Kroehler News of May 10, 1946, "Another citation goes to the kitchen crew led by Ralph (Father) Knickerbocker, "Ma" Jorgensen and Clarence Cather. The Kroehler gang used over 15 pounds of coffee, 50 loaves of bread, and 25 pounds of meat to sustain the tired workers. And at midnight, Ma cooked up 15 gallons of hot turkey soup for them. Helping in the preparation and distribution of all these victuals were Betty Flamming, Bryle Eichelberger, Rose Kaelz, Marilyn Ehrhardt, Marge Yanke, Helen Rechenmacher, Shirley Shroka, Connie Groves, Donna Tait, and Mary Kearns – just to mention a few. Others took care of mothers and their babies who had been brought to the cafeteria."

THE KITCHEN CREW IN THE KROEHLER PLANT worked far into the night making coffee and sandwiches for the tireless workers and the shocked survivors. Those shown in the picture are back row left to right Lillian Shi gut, Rose Kaelz, Connie Groves, Mary Kearns, Shirley Shroka, and Donna Tait. Front row, Laura "Ma" Jorgenson, Beryle Eichelberger, Betty Flamning a nd Helen Rechemacher. The many others who helped could not or would not get into the picture.

Photo from Kroehler Factory News May 10, 1946

Yet another aunt, Helen's and Dick's sister, Bernice Rechenmacher, was attending school at Naperville High School. The high school was located off Washington Street between Spring and Douglas Streets, just a couple of blocks from the accident. Because of the proximity of the school to the accident, students certainly heard the crash and then shortly thereafter all the sirens from the ambulances that were passing by on their way to the wreck. The school went into lock-down mode, but, Bernice remembers, that the curiosity of some of the boys became too much and several of them jumped out their classroom windows and ran over to the site. Dale Flory and Bill Costello, freshmen at the time who were in biology class were two boys who jumped out of their first floor window to run to see the excitement at the Loomis Street crossing.

Audrey Frederickson Murr was a junior and at the time was in Seville Gaston's accounting class on the second floor. Since she was a good student and had finished all her work for the day, Mr. Gaston permitted Audrey to go to the window and watch the ambulance and other emergency vehicles rush to the scene.

At the time of the wreck, Jeanne Clemens (Aeby) was in study hall on the third floor. From that vantage point students could not only hear the loud crash, but could also see a large cloud of dust indicating the site of the accident. Jeanne recalls seeing the flatbed truck carrying the victims as it passed in front of the school. She also remembers that third year student Audrey Peterson, an aid to the school nurse, was the only student who received permission to go to help at the crash scene. In later years Peterson, to Aeby's knowledge, never spoke of her experience.

Sophomore Henry Neyra was in Orville Welzel's gym class that was out on the school's athletic field when the crash occurred. The 1:00pm class had just started when Neyra heard an extremely loud thud. Years later he remembers feeling the ground vibrate and said he also heard a hissing sound that he later figured were the brakes being released. Henry was a young free lance photographer hired by *Naperville Sun* publisher Harold White. As soon as he heard the explosion Henry immediately headed for the locker room where he quickly changed and then proceeded to his school locker to grab the new Speed Graphic camera that White had just purchased for the paper. Neyra then ran through an algebra first floor classroom, jumped out the window, and ran to the accident scene. From 1:10pm to 10pm Henry shot a large number of photographs of the wreck and rescue efforts before he ran out of film. Unfortunately, after six decades and three *Naperville Sun* office moves, just a handful of these photos remain in the newspaper's archives. One of those photos was chosen for the cover of this book.

One of the most impressive stories about the day that Henry can remember has to deal with Frank Johnville, a friend of Neyra's who was an employee of Kroehler but also worked part time at Beidelman's funeral home. During that Thursday Johnville helped load bodies on a flatbed truck for the trip to the funeral home. At one point Frank noticed slight movement from two bodies. These bodies were taken from the truck, given emergency medical attention, and ultimately survived.

Years after the crash, Neyra recalls that the most dramatic incident of the long day took place when the cranes removed the engine of the Exposition Flyer from the last car of the Advance Flyer. The extraction revealed a dead sailor in his full dress summer whites.

It should be noted that Henry Neyra's story conflicts with the account that often has been associated with the *Naperville Sun's* role in documenting the Naperville train tragedy. Sun columnist Genevieve Towsley and some others have claimed that it was Naperville Sun publisher Harold White himself who had the new camera and who took the pictures at the scene. Neyra gives a convincing rendition of his part in the drama. White (d. 1993) and Towsley (d. 1995) are both dead and can give no rebuttal to Neyra's account.

On that same Thursday, C.W. Clark was a patient in St. Charles Hospital in Aurora, Illinois. Clark had already been in the hospital for 18 days. When he heard of the crash, Clark, who was an employee of the Burlington Railroad exclaimed, "Why, that's my train! I'm the brakeman on the Advance. I wonder what happened to my substitute?" Clark's substitute was actually Sherman Grant whose observations ultimately prompted conductor Aue to have the Advance Flyer stopped!

The crash certainly attracted much attention and traffic congestion quickly became a problem. R.N. Givler, Willard Broecker, Howard E. Esser, and Joseph Bapst stepped in to direct traffic at the corner of Washington Street and Jefferson Avenues. After four hours in that capacity they were finally relieved by state police officers.

Charles Weever Cushman, originally from Poseyville, Indiana was from a family of comfortable means. After college he worked for a time as a freight clerk for the Illinois Central Railroad and then enlisted and attained the rank of Seaman 2nd Class in World War I. He went on to a career that included a variety of editorial and managerial positions.

In 1924 he married Elsa Jean Hamilton who was a first cousin to author John Steinbeck. In 1944 Cushman was employed in Chicago by the government to conduct contract termination work.

From 1938 until 1969 Cushman developed a keen interest in photography. After his death in 1972 his collection of 14,500 Kodachrome color slides were bequeathed to his alma mater, Indiana University. The notes from his collection tell us Cushman's activities the day of the train wreck.

Around noontime on April 25th the amateur photographer was snapping pictures of flowers and trees at the Lisle, Illinois Mortem Arboretum. He then, apparently, was startled by the loud explosion from the train collision only a couple miles to the west.

About 15 to 20 minutes later, Cushman was at the Naperville crash site where he took pictures of the wrecked train cars. Despite the devastation before him, Charles, surprisingly, only took seven photographs before returning to the arboretum where his next picture was of an "Acer Palmatum amid Wilson Dwarf Picca and Meyer Juniper". Cushman's photos remain significant because they were among the few color pictures taken of the crash.

Charles W. Cushman took seven color photographs at the crash site. This photograph, which unfortunately had to be rendered into black and white for this book, was taken from the south side of the tracks. The Exposition Flyer can be seen to the right embedded in the Advance Flyer's last car, Northern Pacific #1376. In the foreground is the crumpled mass of the third car from the end, the Silver Inn diner. The photograph (Archived ID: PO 3246) courtesy of the Charles W. Cushman Collection at the Indiana University Archives.

The Kroehler Factory News of May 10, 1946 would later reflect on the tragic scene through the eyes of one of its workers: "Another rescuer, Boney Rieser, told of his first entry into one of the cars. In the center there was a double row of train seats, stacked regularly as if by design, one on top of the other. Here and there between the various seats would project an inert leg, a hand, an arm, or a head. The bodies were wedged in so tightly that parts of the steel work had to be cut away by electric torches before they could be released."

William Marshall Goetz, who was eleven years old at the time of the crash, shares his reflections of that day six decades after the tragedy. He remembered that both of his parents helped at the scene. He also recalls that the impact of the horrible sights they witnessed were both immediate and long lasting.

> *"On this day I remember both my father and my mother, a welder and a nurse, coming home quite late. My father in particular was ashen gray and wouldn't speak. As I recall it, he took a few shots of straight bourbon and went to bed. My mother, perhaps somewhat more inured to carnage from her days in the hospital, explained that there had been a train wreck by the railroad station, a bad one. My dad, and I suppose all the other welders in town, were called upon to bring their cutting torches and cut apart the wreck trying to save as many people as possible and retrieve bodies. My mother was enlisted to help the city's few doctors triage the patients and get them onto transportation to Copley hospital in Aurora and to hospitals in the east."*

The incident was never mentioned after that.

Clyde Erwin was only 16 years old when he enrolled in Naperville's North Central College as a freshman taking a curriculum that emphasized chemistry and math. He lived in a private residence and now shares information that he was not a very conscientious student his first two years of college. Erwin enlisted in the military in 1946, at a time when most people were being discharged after the war. After he returned from service in 1948 he was a much more conscientious student, finished college under the G.I. Bill, and then pursued a law degree.

Clyde remembers that he had just finished his chemistry lab when he heard news of the train wreck. He and some friends ran to the scene and were told that the workers needed an acetylene torch. He and his buddies ran to a welding shop in downtown Naperville and then persuaded the shop owner to lend them a torch that could be used at the crash site. Clyde remembers that he and other college students also went to barrack dorms, stripped beds, and brought mattress frames back to the wreck to be used as stretchers.

Bill Seiser was a freshman at North Central College at the time of the crash. Bill had just finished a class at the college when the loud explosion was heard across the campus. Word quickly spread of the train wreck. Bill ran from class to his nearby home at 204 North Sleight Street to pick up his camera. Seiser's camera was a very small, inexpensive Kodak box camera. He arrived at the scene not long after the wreck had occurred. Bill took about eight pictures of the wreck. He focused on the last three cars, especially car #1376 and the diner car – areas where the damage was most devastating.

North Central College student Bill Seiser captured a dramatic shot of both the destruction of the crash and the dire consequences for a passenger in the last car of the Advance Flyer. Bill Seiser photograph courtesy of North Central College Archives.

Mr. Seiser kept those pictures in a box for 63 years. Then one day he received a visit from Jean Morris, senior associate director of development for North Central. Bill thought of his pictures and asked Jean whether she thought his pictures of that long ago tragedy might still be of some interest to the college.

North Central's archivist, Kim Butler, now wisely asks visitors viewing Mr. Seiser's photographs to wear museum gloves when handling Bill's historic images!

World War II had ended and our military men and women were returning home. Just like after the first world war, our country entered into a period of isolation. America was ready to forget about foreign entanglements; instead, it was ready to be entertained.

In the post war period there was no doubt that baseball would resume its place as our national past time. Some of the greatest players (Feller, DiMaggio, Williams, Spahn, Greenburg, and Musial) had left the sport to join the war effort. Some 500 major leaguers had their careers interrupted by military service (35 of these players eventually would be named to the Hall of Fame). Now these players were returning home to welcoming crowds.

Baseball did not disappoint its faithful disciples. At the beginning of baseball season in April of 1946 several events heightened fans' interest in the game.

On April 14th, Giant player/manager Mel Ott hit the 571st and final home run of his career.

Baseball fans' excitement may have been nowhere as great as in Chicago, as seen by the 40,887 who witnessed the Saturday, April 20th game between the Cubs and the St. Louis Cardinals.

The temperature was 82 degrees, gorgeous weather for a ball game in April. The Cubs were playing their I-55 interstate rivals, the Cardinals. It was early in the season and both teams sported promising 3-1 records. In addition, the contest was an historic one – it was the first televised broadcast of a baseball game in Chicago. The Cardinals won the game 2-0 and ultimately would go on to win the National League pennant.

Baseball continued to be the topic of conversation for the following week. On Tuesday Brooklyn Dodger pitcher Ed Head threw a no-hitter against the Boston Braves in a 5-0 victory.

On Wednesday the Cubs keystone combination of Tinker, Evers, and Chance were elected together into baseball's Hall of Fame.

It is most certain that on Thursday, April 25, 1946, there were a good number of Naperville residents who were, for most of the day, oblivious to the tragic proceedings that were taking place in their town. Instead, they were at a ball game at Chicago's Wrigley Field.

On that Thursday the Cincinnati Reds were in Chicago for just a single game against the Chicago Cubs. It would, therefore, be a very limited opportunity for family and friends to witness the skills of thirty-two year old native son, Bert Haas, who played first base for the Reds baseball team.

Haas would play nine years in the big leagues (between 1937-1951) with stints with the Dodgers (2 years); Reds (4 years); Phillies (1 year); Giants (1 year); and White Sox (1 year).

Bert wore number "18" and played first base for the Cincinnati team. Although his team beat the Cubs 7-5 that day, Haas was not able to display his batting skills for his hometown fans as he went hitless in five at bats.

The memories of a pleasant day at the ballpark for Haas' supporters quickly were overshadowed on the return trip to Naperville by the shocking news of the tragic train wreck. The May 2nd edition of the *Naperville Sun* reported that a Naperville resident attending the Cubs game heard of the train wreck when leaving the ballpark. That unidentified person stated that, at the time, he was not able to connect with anyone from Naperville because of jammed phone lines.

☆　☆　☆

On the fiftieth anniversary of the train wreck, *Daily Herald* reporter Lorilyn Rackl recorded the reflections of Floyd Thompson, who was also a North Central College student at the time of the crash:

"I was taking a midterm exam at North Central College. I started hearing the sirens and saw people running north. I couldn't control myself. I told the professor 'I've lived in town all my life and the most exciting thing that ever happened was when my cat died.' He let me go. I ran as fast as I could. When I got there, it was an indescribable mess – trains piled all over, people hanging out windows. I couldn't believe what had happened."

In that same 1996 news article Rackl reported the thoughts of Naperville resident Herb Matter who heard about the crash while he was in the military and stationed in Germany. Matter said that he had to pinch himself when he saw the headlines in *The Stars and Stripes*, "Naperville, Illinois. Scene of Train Wreck that Kills 47".

☆ ☆ ☆

Those dead and seriously injured taken from the North side of the train were taken to a temporary morgue set up in the Kroehler factory. Many of the dead bodies were covered with white paper that normally would be used to wrap Kroehler furniture products. Table cloths from the diner car of the Exposition Flyer were also used to shroud the bodies. Many of the injured on the South side of the tracks were taken temporarily taken to homes on Fourth Avenue or were laid on the ground until emergency vehicles could transport them to Aurora hospitals. Cots and mattresses from Merner Field House were brought to the scene by North Central college students and seminarians.

Calista Wehrli got aggravated with the rubber neckers who were hindering relief efforts. At one point, when she couldn't move a stretcher through a crowd, she cursed at the crowd and

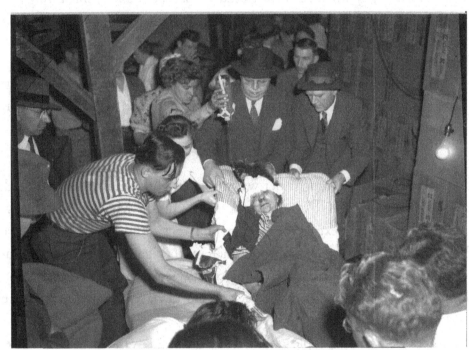

An injured elderly woman has received on-site emergency care and is now being carried to an ambulance for transport to an Aurora hospital. The author believes the woman is Anne Hovey, the Marine nurse holding the IV is Calista Wehrli, and the hospital of destination is St. Charles. Photograph courtesy of Paul Hinterlong.

commanded the mass of people to pass the stretcher over their heads to either homes or ambulances or cars that were transporting the injured to hospitals in nearby Aurora, seven miles away. Calista again became agitated when she accompanied an injured woman in an ambulance to a hospital in Aurora. The ambulance was forced to travel on the westbound berm of the road because both traffic lanes were taken up with the cars of curiosity seekers traveling eastbound to Naperville to examine the site of the crash.

Calista, as was mentioned, was working closely with Jack Meluch. Later Meluch recalled working to free a woman who had spent a long time trapped in a car. She was hanging upside down with a heel caught in the overhead luggage rack. When workers finally were able to extricate her, the lady refused to be carried out on a stretcher. Her decision proved to be a fatal one as, after she had taken a few steps, she fell unconscious. Efforts to revive her were unsuccessful.

At the time of the crash, Naperville had two weekly newspapers, the *Naperville Sun* and the *Naperville Clarion*. Just as the crash occurred one of the Sun's reporters, Ferne Hoeft, was leaving for work. She lived a block away from the accident. Instead of heading for the office, Hoeft rushed to the crash site. In her article written for the United Press, Ferne made the following statement:

> *"When I was running toward the trains from the south, across the highway I came upon the body of a man. He looked like he had been one of the dining car workers, for his coat was white. He was lying there all alone, where someone had carried him. A fellow with me covered the dead man with his coat."*

Looking at the last coach, car #1376, she recorded "I could see people sticking out of the windows. A part of a leg dropped from the window of the coach. There were moans and cries."

JoAnn Martin Baumgartner was in Sister Alphonsetta's second grade classroom at Saints Peter and Paul School when the train wreck occurred. The Martins' house was at 324 N. Ellsworth Street, a big yellow house next to the Naperville paper stand just around the corner from Fourth Avenue. When she came home from school, her mother gave her instructions to stay at home and not to venture anywhere near the site of the train wreck. JoAnn's curiosity got the best of her and before long she had disappeared out the back door and was on Fourth Avenue, in front of the Widder house at 252 Fourth Avenue.

There were many people gathered along the sidewalk and as she moved forward for a better look, she noticed the bodies of some of the injured laying on the tree lawns waiting for ambulances to take them for treatment. In fact, as she moved up through the crowd, she was startled to see right below her a black porter in uniform. He was bleeding from the head and JoAnn thought how vivid the red blood was against the dark skin. The man's navy jacket was at his side. The man was very still and quiet. She backed away from this sight but was to remember the image quite vividly 64 years later when this author interviewed her.

There were adults who tried to shoo away the many children who had gathered at the scene. Their efforts were mainly in vain since most of the attention and energy was focused on the rescue efforts taking place before them.

As JoAnn looked across at the wrecked trains, she focused in on a figure standing on top of an overturned car. Joanne didn't know it at the time, but this car was the Silver Cloud. What she did know was that the man on the train helping to extracate the injured from the wreck was her father, John Martin. Her dad was one of those many workers from Kroehler who had run to help at the scene.

It wasn't long before JoAnn's mother came looking for her daughter. Her mother was furious that JoAnn had gone to the crash site and she quickly took her home. Through the years JoAnn would wonder about the fate of that black porter and wished at times she would have said something that might have consoled him. Her memory "instilled the vivid realization of how narrow the passage is from existence to death".

Adding to the intrigue and mystic of the crash scene was the presence of four aircraft circling the area. One of these planes was a civilian version of the famous C-47 (formerly known as the DC-3 before the war). The C-47 was used in the battles of Guadalcanal, New Guinea, and Bastogne. The plane's fame increased when it was used to fly "The Hump" from India to China. It later was to be employed in the Berlin Airlift and as a gunship in the Vietnam War.

The photographs taken from these planes provided some excellent historical perspective and documentation for the Naperville rail tragedy.

There was a very small number of survivors from the last car of the Advance Flyer. Perhaps the names of Raymond Jaeger, Irene Cook, Florence Whitehouse, Anne Hovey, Sol Greenbaum, Reverend Dunstan Velesz, and Henry and Edith Faber may well complete the list.

Mrs. Irene Cook, her mother, Mrs. Florence Whitehouse, and the woman they pledged to care for along the way – Mrs. Anne Hovey – were all relaxing in the rear car at the time of the accident. Twenty year old Mrs. Cook was the youngest of the three travelers and was seated facing the back of the car.

Ignoring her mother's instructions, second grader JoAnn Baumgartner visited the scene of the wreck. In 2011 JoAnn is shown standing at the same location on Fourth Ave. where, as a young child, she had viewed the injured passengers and the wreckage. Photograph taken by author.

"I was seated facing the approaching train, but it all happened so fast I didn't see it clearly. Suddenly I must have been thrown into the air, because I remember hitting the seat twice with my head and waking up under a pile of people and seats. My mother was buried beneath another man and a woman. I could see my mother's hat. I begged her to speak to

me. She said her legs were twisted and bleeding. There was so much screaming that I was as frightened when rescued as when the crash occurred. The men came with their torches through the top of the car and sparks fell. We were afraid they would ignite oil in the car. One of my legs was caught under something, but I pulled it free and went around putting out the sparks as they fell. Even before the rescuers started working we were frightened by the smell of the ashes. I was taken out of a window, but I haven't yet heard what happened to my mother."

As it turned out, Irene would not learn the fate of her mother for some time, because while Irene was taken to St. Charles Hospital in Aurora for treatment, her mother was at Aurora's Copley Hospital where she had a leg amputated. Fortunately, as was stated earlier, at the time of the crash, there was a full staff of 50 doctors and 77 nurses and student nurses at the St. Charles Hospital attending a weekly staff meeting.

After the crash, seventy-two-year-old Anne Hovey recalled that "things happened so fast that I don't remember what happened to me. I was doubled up suddenly and my knees were pushed against my chest." Because of this sudden compression, both of Anne Hovey's legs were fractured and she was unconscious when rescue workers carried her from the wreckage. Ultimately, all three women would survive, but Mrs. Hovey would not be released from the hospital until six months later. Anne was one of the last three patients from the wreck to be released from St. Charles Hospital.

Sol Greenbaum had stirred a little from his nap as the Advance Flyer came to its unscheduled stop in Naperville. Instead of being crushed like many of the other passengers in car #1376, Sol later related "When the crash came I was thrown to the top of the car, turned a somersault and came down. A pile of people fell on me. I kicked out a window and climbed out. I think a woman behind me was killed."

Henry Faber, 27, discharged on Monday from the Marines, had survived rugged Pacific Island battles. Although he and his wife, Edith, 29, were to survive the Naperville crash, they did not come out unscathed. Both spouses had their shoes torn from their feet and their clothes were shredded beyond repair. They both had blackened eyes and multiple cuts and bruises.

Faber would later relate: "I didn't think I'd make it through the war. My regiment went over on four ships and came back in one compartment. I went through all that in the Pacific only to come home and have this happen. We were in the rear car and our seats faced foreword. I got up to put my coat in the (overhead) rack and looked back to see the other train coming." There was nothing to do but sit down. Edith related that "the feeling of suffocation was worst of all. I couldn't breathe. My legs were pinned behind me. I was doubled up like a jackknife." Mrs. Faber would remain in that position for two hours before she was freed.

After they were freed from the wreckage, the Fabers were treated at St. Charles Hospital. The patient in the bed next to the Henry Faber was Exposition Flyer engineer William Blaine.

Riding in the Silver Cloud, the fourth car from the end of the train was Wesley "Blaine" Overman who was returning home to Caldwell, Idaho. Blaine had decided to wait to eat until the train reached Omaha. His decision to avoid the diner car may well have saved his life. Also in the Silver Cloud was Navy man George Whitney, returning home after four years of service in the military. Sitting right behind Overman was a woman with a very small baby. Upon the terrible impact from the crash, the baby flew from the mother's arms and into the air. Fortunately, Whitney caught the baby in mid air and was able to protect it even though several other people, jostled from the crash fell on top of George and the baby. Because of the collision the Silver Cloud derailed and landed on its side. Overman remembered there was an accessible window in the washroom. Blaine was able to open this window, and one of the first persons handed out the window was the baby Whitney had saved. The baby was handed to Kroehler yard foreman, Harold Schrader. Because the baby was so well bundled up, Schrader did not know whether it was a boy or a girl. He does remember that he held it for a while until the mother was able to be freed from the train. He vividly remembered that the mother was most anxious to be reunited with her baby and could be excused for never thanking Harold for his assistance. Through the succeeding years, Schrader would often wonder about the baby's whereabouts and well being.

Not only did George Whitney save a baby that day, but, in his own words, "I helped carry 17 bodies out of the train. It was worse than anything I ever saw in war!"

After he got free of the train, Overman realized that there were plenty of rescue help at the crash site. His thoughts then became focused on how to hitch hike home. However, none of the people he talked with knew the route that would get him out of town and that would link him to a major western traffic system.

He then met someone who told him that an auxiliary replacement train would be coming from Chicago and would stop at the Naperville depot to pick up passengers. Wesley went to the train station to wait for

Blaine Overman and George Whitney managed to open a window in the restroom of the overturned Silver Cloud and help lift passengers out to safety. Bill Seiser photograph courtesy of North Central College Archives.

his ride. The replacement train took Overman to Omaha where he completed his journey home aboard the Portland Rose.

When that auxiliary train arrived, a Burlington representative went around looking for persons who had suffered some injury as a result of the wreck. Blaine had scrapped his shin and the representative brought him a bandage, gave him $25 in compensation, and then had him sign a waiver of liability. Mr. Overman indicated that he tried unsuccessfully to refuse compensation.

Sometimes a sudden, terrifying, life-threatening event has people acting a bit outside their normal parameters. Such was the case for Mrs. W.A. Grubb of Marysville, Pennsylvania. Mrs. Grubb stated to reporters after the crash that "I was riding on the third car from the rear of the train that was hit. About all I can remember is the crash and the sensation of the car tipping over. It seemed like hours before the car finally plunged over on its side. Some soul, I don't have any idea who he was, offered me a drink of whiskey, and I surprised myself by taking it." If the car Mrs. Grubb was in tipped over on its side, and since she was going to Lincoln, Nebraska, then she was definitely riding in the fourth car from the rear (the Silver Cloud), not the third. Had she been riding in the third car (the dining car, the Silver Inn), it is very likely she would have been killed or seriously injured. Was Mrs. Grubb's statement distorted because of the intensity of the situation or did that gulp of whiskey cloud her memory? Actually observers on the scene could well be excused for mistaking the order of the train cars after the accident because the cars were scattered and the diner (Silver Inn) was turned back around and nearly totally demolished.

During the short ride from Chicago, there certainly was much action on the Silver Inn, the Advance Flyer's dining car. The chefs and waiters were right in the midst of their lunch service.

When the train stopped in Naperville, second cook LaValle E. Neal told his boss, Don Donegan, that he was going to go see what the problem was. Neal thought the Advance Flyer was on a siding waiting for the Exposition Flyer to pass. When Neal saw the Exposition Flyer round the bend, he knew his train was in terrible trouble. He yelled for everyone to jump.

Three waiters, Daniel Carr, Charles Butler, and Charles Chamberlain all died in the crash. A fourth waiter, William McBride, later affirmed that the actions of Daniel Carr saved his life. "When the car started to collapse, Daniel Carr caught one of the walls that would have crushed me to death. I fell under his legs. When I crawled out, Carr was dead...Carr's arm was torn from his body, and he kept the pantry wall off me. That is how I was prevented from being killed."

Chief cook, Don Donegan, was the father of the famous boogie-woogie queen, Dorothy Donegan. In her memoirs recorded by Whitney Balliett in the story entitled "Wonder Woman", Dorothy writes of her parents:

> *"My mother was a sometime domestic, and my father was a chef-cook with the C.B.&Q – the Chicago, Burlington, and Quincy Railroad. He loved to play the trumpet, but he was a better cook. He cooked that rice and gravy and fried chicken, and when he did a turkey he used milk and butter and wrapped it in cheese cloth and cooked it into submission. He worked forty years on the railroad, and he died in 1958, a stroke. He was tall and brown-skinned and handsome, but his head was smaller than his body. I think he had Indian*

blood. He loved cards – bridge and whist – and he'd cuss in a loud voice if he lost. He had come up to Chicago from Huntsville, Alabama, around 1916. That was where Tallulah Bankhead was from, Speaker Bankhead's daughter? His name was Donazell – Donazell Donegan. That's a curious name, but nobody's perfect."

Julius McCloud, a waiter, was setting up a tray of sandwiches for some servicemen in the diner when the crash occurred. McCloud was taken to the hospital for back pain and treatment for shock.

Most of the diner car, the Silver Inn, like most of the last car, #1376, was heavily damaged. Most of the passengers who died were from one of those two cars. William McBride stated that "the whole kitchen was messed up like scrambled eggs." Actually, the kitchen itself, toward the front of the car, had some construction protection and fewer people died in that area than in the general dining area.

Rescue crews attempt to remove the dead and injured from car #1376. A member of the dining crew looks on from inside that same last car. It appears that a bucket of preloaded morphine syringes is on the scaffolding that Kroehler workers erected next to the wrecked car. Bill Seiser photograph courtesy of North Central College Archives.

Mr. and Mrs. John A. Sromovsky of Wilkes-Barre, Pennsylvania, were in the Silver Inn eating soup at the time of the collision. The impact of the crash caused their soup to fly in the couple's faces. Sophie Sromovsky would die 10 hours after the wreck. She suffered from a fractured skull, and leg and wrist injuries. Sergeant Sromovsky also suffered injuries from the crash, but he refused morphine that was offered him as he was being taken from the site. "Other people need it worse than I do." Sromovsky told a rescue worker. The flagman for train #39, C.W. Norris related that "I saw a doctor climbing on top of one of #11's cars, which was turned over on its side, and reach down through a window to give a woman a hypo. She was screaming."

Wilbert "Wib" Bauer was a Kroehler employee who also happened to be the Red Cross' first-aid instructor for DuPage County. He certainly played a crucial part in administering initial, on site help to those injured in the wreck. Wib's son, Jim, clearly remembers his dad relating to him incidents like those mentioned above that involved the Sromovskys and C.W. Norris:

> *"When the train wreck occurred, Kroehlers shut down and used their trucks to help out by transporting the deceased to the temporary morgue staging area set up at North Central College's field house. Dad went to help out at the wreck site administering morphine hypos to the victims. I remember him saying that they were given mop buckets full of preloaded syringes and told to inject any part of a body that they could see. He said a lot of the victims were hidden with only a part of the body visible. They were told that unless it was an obvious dismemberment, to inject anything visible….there was a snapshot of my father, leaning out of a train window exchanging a bucket of syringes. We've misplaced the picture unfortunately."*

Like the Sromovskys, Council Bluff residents Thomas Chaney and Fred Robinson were enjoying lunch when the wreck occurred. Robinson would lose his life in the accident. Chaney was hospitalized for quite some time. In fact, he was one of the last two people to be released from the hospital due to injuries suffered in the Naperville wreck. Thomas suffered from a fractured pelvis and a broken jaw. Both an ear and a leg were sheared off in the wreck and his bladder was punctured.

It is highly likely that Mrs. Charlotte Collins was eating in the diner at the time of the crash. She was another of the crash fatalities. Her son-in-law had taken her to the train in the morning and later stated that at the time of the wreck, Mrs. Collins was seated in a car in the middle of the train. Since Carlotte's destination was Hannibal, Missouri, it was most likely that she started out in car #1376, the last car in the Advance Flyer. If, after the crash, a relative mentioned that she had been in the middle car, then Mrs. Collins must have ventured to the diner car, the Silver Inn. From either car, her chances of survival were slim and her funeral was to be one of a number where there was a closed casket. Mrs. Collins body was identified on Friday morning by her daughter and son-in-law, Mr. and Mrs. C.N. Hultberg of Highland Park, Illinois.

Businessmen John N. Ralson and Al N. Miller would never make it to their business trip to Canton, Missouri. Both men were killed in the crash. Ralson would leave his wife Rita and eight children (five sons and three daughters); Miller would leave his wife, Irene, and two children, four-year old Ellen Irene and two-year old John Wayne. Al's brother Henry came to Naperville to identify his brother's body. Al's parents would lose another of their six sons in 1946. Elmer Miller died that same year at Hine's Veteran Hospital in Maywood, Illinois of injuries he incurred in the war.

Although only 30 at the time of her husband's death, Irene Miller would never remarry. She became an accountant at The Harris Bank in Chicago where she had a long and successful career.

Matt Lawrence Jr. identified the bodies of his parents who were both killed in the train wreck. Mr. and Mrs. Matt L. Lawrence Sr. were on their way to visit their son in Ottumua, Iowa.

Lt. Colonel Daniel J. Moss came to Napeville from Galesburg, Illinois to identify the bodies of his parents, Dr. and Mrs. Leo P. Moss, both of whom died in the crash.

Thirty-five-year-old, recently discharged soldier Everett Eugene Conner from South Bend, Indiana, wouldn't get to surprise his father in Hannibal, Missouri. Everett was crushed to death in car #1376. Conner was survived by his wife, Helen.

At the time of the crash, Elves King had been living in Chicago and was employed as the general manger of a corset company. Elves had been traveling to Bloomington, Illinois to attend a business meeting.

King was in the last car of the Advance Flyer. After the crash the identity of the sixty-nine year old was made possible only through his name that was engraved on his wrist watch.

Elves was survived by two daughters, Barbara and Marianne who were both married to Army officers. King's death also left a son, Elves Jr. The son had the following epitaph engraved on his father's tombstone which can be found in Pine Valley Cemetery in LaPorte, Indiana:

TO MY FATHER THERE IS NONE BETTER

Emma Schuetz never made it to help take care of her sick grandchildren. She was in the badly mangled last car and her body was able to be identified only by rings that she was wearing. This was the second time that tragedy had befallen the Schuetz family. In 1933 Emma's husband, Louis Schuetz, a security guard, had been shot to death in a murder that never was solved.

Harry Long was another military man who had recently been discharged and another one of the victims who was engaged and would soon have been married. Shot down four times during the war, his life would be taken in the train wreck. Harry Long's luck ran out on April 25th, 1946.

One of the sadder stories of the crash belongs to Delbert Boon. He was scheduled to be discharged from military service in June to return to the tranquility of the family farm about seven miles northeast of Luray, Missouri. Delbert was seriously injured in the crash and taken to St. Charles Hospital in Aurora, Illinois. Delbert requested that someone send a telegram to his parents. The telegram read "Come and see me. Was in train accident." Then, Delbert handed his dog-tags to a nun and asked that she give the items to his mother "with all my love". He then requested a priest. Father Robert Buckley administered the last rites to Boon. Delbert's parents certainly had false hopes when they received that telegram, because Delbert died thirty minutes after the message was sent.

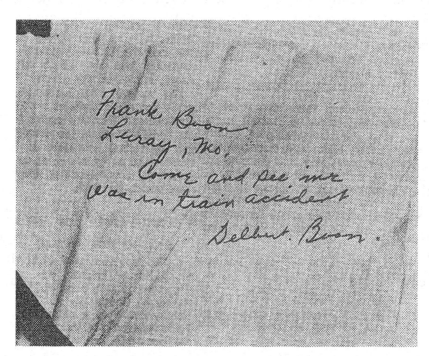

Delbert Boon's message that he asked to have sent to his parents. Unfortunately, Delbert died thirty minutes after the telegram was sent. Chicago Tribune photograph.

*Delbert Boon is buried in Chambersburg Methodist Cemetery in
Jefferson Township, Missouri. The inscription on the tombstone reads:*

*"Fireman First Class
Delbert F. Boon,
Born Mar. 30, 1925
Served aboard USS Attala, U.S.N., WWII
Killed in Train Wreck, Naperville, Ill
Apr. 25, 1946"*

Photograph taken by Rodney Harvey.

The day was filled with tragic stories of those who died and how their passing affected the families they left behind. One of those stories was of Joe Bentler another victim from car #1376. Mr. Bentler, whose wife died in 1937 left 11 children, four of whom were still at home.

Although a nursing student herself, twenty-three year old Lucy Takashima couldn't be nursed back to health. She died Friday morning from head injuries, compound fractures of both legs, and other assorted serious ailments.

☆ ☆ ☆

Henry and Rosa Voss, the parents of Bernard Voss, along with Bernard's financee, Miss Bernice Klauser, certainly were filled with tremendous anxiety when word was delayed in reaching them Thursday concerning Bernard's fate. They were elated certainly with the news of Bernard's discharge from the service on Tuesday. Bernard and Beatrice had intended to formally announce their engagement on Sunday, the 28th.

However, the anxious group's worst fears were realized when word finally came from Naperville on Friday that Bernard was among the victims whose bodies were identified. It was difficult to identify many of the crash victims, and in Bernard's case, identification was aided by the initials on a fountain pen found among the effects of the body.

☆ ☆ ☆

Passenger Reverend Dunstan Velesz was credited with providing a calming influence to the otherwise physical anguish, confusion, and disorientation that passengers felt in the last car.

"I was in the last coach near the front of the car, when the train drew to a halt. I saw a trainman run through the car to the rear, as if to stop the approaching train. I expected a freight train to pass. Suddenly there was a terrific crash. I felt myself being pushed forward. Seats began to accordion imprisoning screaming humans between them. Seats and bodies were pushed to the ceiling. A girl (Irene Cook) screamed to her mother and begged her to answer. Prayers mingled with the cries. I tried to free myself but could not move my legs. I was pinned down. The priest heard the agonized cry, "Oh Lord have mercy!" *I began to pray aloud, and some joined me. I gave conditional absolution to all."*

Despite injuring one of his legs, Father Velesz stayed at the accident scene for about a half hour administering comfort, soothing words, and the last rites to fellow passengers in the last car. He finally left after three priests, Fathers Frederick R. Stenger, Charles Koretke, and Paul Benson replaced him at the site. It was Father Stenger's very first year as pastor of SS. Peter and Paul Church in Naperville. Among his 24 years at the parish, few days would be as memorable as this one – one of his very first at his new assignment.

View from south side of tracks looking east. Bill Seiser photo shows three Catholic priests at the crash site. Reverends Frederick R. Stenger, Paul Benson, and Charles Koretke from SS Peter and Paul parish, along with visiting priests Reverends Leonard Matter and James Quinn, administered last rights to the victims. Bill Seiser photograph courtesy of North Central College Archives.

70

☆　☆　☆

After taking his wife and two young sons to Union Station, Alfred Wiley returned to work at the Electro Motive Corporation plant in LaGrange, Illinois. It was just a short time later that Wiley heard on the radio of the Naperville train wreck. He borrowed a friend's car, left work immediately, and arrived at the train site at approximately 3:15pm. Unable to locate his family there, Wiley spent several hours phoning the three Aurora hospitals in the desperate hopes of finding word that his wife and boys were alive. In between the calls he visited the three local mortuaries where the victims of the crash were being taken. An exhausted Mr. Wiley was at the Charles Frederick Funeral Home at 44 South Mill Street when three final victims, his family, were brought from the accident site. It was 6:30pm. His agony was obviously beyond description. Since no other baby has been reported on death records, it is highly likely that the year old Randy Wiley was the crushed baby found near its decapitated mother whom we also speculate to have been Maralyn Wiley. Again, Randy and his three-year old brother Terry most assuredly were the boys Rosie Hodel saw crushed to death against the window of the last train car.

Ironically, the Electro-Motive Corporation where Alfred Wiley worked assembled the motors like the Silver Speed and the Silver Power that telescoped into the Advance Flyer.

Funeral home personnel load the caskets of Maralyn Wiley and her two sons, Terry and Randy for shipment to the Giles Funeral Home in Burlington, Iowa. Interment was at Aspen Grove Cemetery. Photograph courtesy of Paul Hinterlong.

☆　☆　☆

A very active and engaging life both with her family and with her community came to a sudden, tragic end on April 25th for Mrs. Mary Langen. The Langen family had traveled from Quincy, Illinois to Chicago for an Easter visit with friends and family. Mary decided to stay in Chicago a few days after other members in her party left for back home. Mary was taking advantage of Chicago's stores to pick up items for her family and her home. The decision cost Langen her life and she left behind a husband, C.S. Langen, a son, John, and a daughter, Mary Lou.

Another act of kindness also turned out to result in the loss of life of Mrs. Kay Lummis Flotkoetter, 22, of Chicago. Other family members had traveled to Quincy, Illinois on Wednesday to attend the Saturday wedding of Robert Flotkoetter, Kay's brother-in-law. Mrs. Flotkoetter stayed behind to help a friend who had just given birth. Her one day delay was made permanent by the tragic crash. Kay, 22, left behind her husband, Charles.

Yet another of the soldiers involved in Thursday's crash was 19 year old, Richard Edwin Howard. The young 19 year old Gunner's Mate 3rd class USNR had followed his father's call to service with the Navy. The elation his parents Leander and Ray Howard felt back in Stillwell, Iowa upon first hearing of their son's discharge on Tuesday was muted when positive identification of the body was finally forthcoming.

Mrs. Florence Wilson was traveling to Burlington, Iowa. Therefore, she was directed to car #1376. During the train's short trip before it stopped in Naperville, Florence decided to go to the diner car. Unfortunately, neither seat designation would be of help in saving her life. Most of the victims of the train wreck were seated in either the last car or the diner. Florence and her professor husband, Harold were together in Chicago Wednesday. That was the last time they would see each other as Harold headed for the University of Minnesota and Florence headed for a visit with her family in Birmingham, Iowa, approximately 45 miles west of Burlington. Florence, who was in her mid 40's left her husband, but no children.

Clifford Yarbrough unfortunately was also in car #1376 on April 25th, 1946. At age 58 he was a veteran, but with a longer military resume than the other military personnel riding on either train that day. Yarbrough survived the U.S. conflict with Mexico, World War I, and civilian service in the Pearl Harbor shipyards in World War II. But, he could not survive the collision in Naperville. Clifford had never married. A brother and sister survived him.

Occasionally in the crash, death took a random swipe at passengers who sat side by side. It took Fred Robinson not Tom Chaney; it took Sophie Sromovsky instead of her husband John; and it took sailor Howard Stimpson instead of his traveling companion, Army Pvt. Elbert Hartman. Twenty-two-year-old Hartman was seated on the aisle which seemed to have given passengers the availability of some open space when the seats were crushed together. Stimpson, seated by the window did not have this luxury and consequently was not lucky enough to survive the crash.

Stimpson's death brought a tragic end to what started as a very bright day. That very morning he was discharged from the Great Lakes Naval Center after three years of service to his country. Most of his tour was in the Pacific and he had come through his ordeal without a scratch.

Hartman later reflected that

"Howard and I were just sitting there talking and wondering why the train had stopped when I felt a big jolt and everything was thrown to the front of the car. When we settled down again I looked around and saw the prong of another train engine sticking into the rear of our car. Our car was split right down the middle and people were all squeezed between and under seats. There was quite a bit of screaming by the women on the car who were hurt. I just can't understand how I came through it like I did".

As was stated, Pvt. Hartman survived with only a bruise on his arm due to the fact that he had an aisle seat and that he was seated near the front of the rear car. Some consolation was given to Stimpson's father Robert of Carmen, Illinois, when Hartman reported that his travel companion had not lingered in death, but had died instantly.

The *Hawkeye Gazette* would write several stories about the Naperville train wreck. This tragedy was more than just a news story to the editor of the Gazette's weekly labor column, P.L. Mennen whose wife Mayme died in the crash. Mayme was quite an active and independent lady who had visited friends and relatives in Florida, Indianapolis, and Chicago before returning home to Burlington, Iowa. Mr. Mennen did not learn of the crash until he went to the Burlington station to pick up his wife. He then would continue to return to meet each train that Thursday afternoon and evening frantically searching for news about his wife's fate. Mayme's death would not be confirmed until Friday morning. Mrs. Mennen's death would be a blow to the many organizations she served in her community; but, most especially, she would be missed by her husband and their adopted son John.

Mayme's funeral was one that, at one time, was not uncommon, but today is never seen. Her wake was held at the Mennen's own residence. Mayme's body was prepared at the Giles Funeral Home, then was taken to the family's home on Saturday afternoon. The rosary was recited at the house in the evening by the Daughters of Isabella. On Monday there was a short service at the house at 8:30am. Then the funeral mass was held at St. Patrick's Catholic Church at 9am. The funeral procession then journeyed from the church to the cemetery for final burial services.

A second victim of the crash who had connections with the Hawk-eye Gazette was Russell Whitehead, 34, of Weymouth, Massachusetts. Russell and his wife, Eleanor, 35, also a fatality in the the crash, were traveling to Burlington, Iowa where Mr. Whitehead had accepted employment as a linotype operator for the Gazette.

It was learned that the Whiteheads were among the passengers who were in the dining car (Silver Inn) at the time of the crash.

Russell Whitehead's body was identified immediately, but Eleanor was not listed among the fatalities until Friday. The E.B. Black Funeral Home in Hereford, Texas, sent Matt Gilliland to return Mr. Whitehead's body to his hometown for burial. The body of Mrs. Whitehead, born Eleanor Burke, was returned to Boston for burial near her hometown of Weymouth.

The couple had one son, Charles Homer Whitehead, a child that Russell had from a previous marriage.

Hiram Stebbins was suppose to be in the last car, #1376, but had opted instead to sit with a friend he found in a more comfortable car in the Silver Gleam. When conductor, J.E. Aue checked Hiram's ticket he told Stebbins he would have to move back to a seat in the last car. Stebbins, citing empty seats and promising to get off in Burlington, convinced conductor Aue to let him stay where he was seated. Stebbins' life was spared.

It is said of some employees that they will never retire and will eventually die on the job. That fate ended up as proving true for August Anderson, a 43 year employee of the Burlington railroad. Anderson was 68 years old and would leave a wife, Helen, and two sons.

The train wreck was so horrific that identification of victims often times could only be made through clothing, physical characteristics, or jewelry. That was the case with twenty-two year old Mrs. Dorothy Aman. William Aman was able to identify his wife only through a description of her clothing (light blue-green dress), a diamond ring, a class ring given to her by her husband, and a scar on her leg. Dorothy was in the early stages of pregnancy. Most readers of this book would picture Mrs. Aman's fetus as an unborn. This author can only picture what the life of that child would be like today had it survived to adulthood – for the age of Mrs. Aman's baby and the age of this author would have been identical!

Lieutenant Kenneth Dickhut was patriotic, ambitious, and dedicated. These last two qualities might have resulted in his death in the Naperville crash. Lt. Dickhut was urged by his brother Harold to extend his visit with him in Chicago for several more days. Instead, Kenneth decided to return to Quincy so that he could study for his certified public accountant examination. The 30 year old Dickhut had served his country for four and a half years in the recent war and had now been eager to wed his fiance, Miss Irene Marcotte and to start a new career. War had spared him, but because of the tragic events of April 25th, a promising future was denied this renaissance man with music as an avocation. Dickhut was survived by his mother, Mrs. Emma Dickhut and his brother Harold.

Another train fatality, Edward Reed Sherwood, was recently discharged from the Naval Reserve and just moved from New Orleans to Chicago. Edward would never see where his great training and talent would take him next. Edward left behind his wife, Catherine Ernst and an eight year old son, Edward R. Sherwood Jr.

The relatives of Marion Brickman Craft still had not received word of Marion's fate as they waited at the Quincy, Illinois rail station Thursday and Friday. Her body was one of the last to be identified. The young bride had been on her way to pay a final visit to her father, Walter Brickman, who, she had been told, was on the verge of death. The devastating news of Marion's death was finally received back at Quincy after Marion's husband, Sergeant Glenn Craft traveled to Naperville and identified his wife's body. Relatives at the station were shocked and heart broken – for Marion and her father had both died on that Thursday, April 25th. On Monday a double funeral was held for father and daughter. The anguish Sergeant Craft certainly felt was made even less bearable upon his return to the North Chicago. When Glenn checked the mail, he discovered that the couple's wedding pictures had been delivered to the apartment during his absence!

Anyone who saw the destruction of the dining car knew that the dining steward, Arthur Abbott had little chance of surviving the crash. Upon hearing the tragic news , Arthur's wife and two children, June Rae and Arthur Raymond Jr. returned from a trip to Minocqua, Wisconsin to make funeral arrangements in Berwyn.

Unfortunately, Mary Farley became a fatality of the crash as she also was in the dining car. Her body was identified by L.G. Lamais, president of Mary's place of employment, Lyon and Healy in Chicago. Records indicate that Mary was administered the last rites at St. Charles Hospital by Reverend Robert Buckley.

Abraham and Elizabeth Rohr (75 and 72 years old respectively) were on their way to Omaha, Nebraska to visit their daughter Hannah and her husband Charles. Their destination would mean that they were directed to seats in either the Silver Cloud or the Silver Gleam where there were no record of fatalities. This would indicate that the Rohr's were eating lunch in the Silver Inn dining car at the time of the crash. Their bodies were only able to be identified through the use of dental records. The elderly couple would leave behind two grown daughters, Hannah (Honey) and Sadie.

Elza Lett Jr., twenty-five years old had been married to the U.S. Army for four years. He never got the chance to marry and be part of the generation that would produce the post war baby boom. His death eliminated the possibility of extending his family heritage to an Elza Lett III.

★ ★ ☆

At 6:00pm on April 25, 1946, John "Jack" Lane, as was his custom, walked down to the local drugstore to pick up the Chicago Daily News for the family. At the time there was no home delivery in the area of the Lane residence at 7519 Claremont Avenue in Chicago. Jack was a seventeen-year-old high school senior who, in a few short weeks, would be graduating from Loyola Academy.

Jack, along with his nineteen-year-old sister, Mary Claire, lived with their parents, Albert and Hazel (Heelan) Lane. His father's mother, Clara Belle Lane, also lived at the residence.

This day the clerk at the drugstore gave Jack an unusual request. He made Jack promise that he would fold the paper and not open it until he returned home. The store clerk had seen the paper's headlines about the train wreck in Naperville and had, more importantly, also seen Albert Lane's picture in the paper as one of the victims of the crash. The clerk wanted Jack to be with family when he learned of his father's death.

Jack obeyed the order given him. Two visitors to the Lane house beat Jack there by about five minutes. Clem Lane (no relationship to the Albert Lane family), lived directly across the street from Jack and his family. Clem Lane was also the city editor of *The Chicago Daily News*. Because of his position, Clem knew early on of Albert's death and decided that he would try to console his neighbors when he came home from work. Nearly six hours after the crash his neighbors had not yet learned of Albert's death. One must realize that, without TV, word of local and national news events traveled much slower in those days. Clem thought it best that on the way home he'd pick up and bring with him Father Gilmore, a priest from St. Margaret Mary parish. Those two men were at Jack's house when he returned with the paper. And those two men broke the news to the family of the death of Hazel's husband, Clara Belle's son, and Jack and Mary Claire's father.

Jack Lane stands in the patio of his Park Ridge, Illinois home after his interview with the author. Jack was seventeen years old and just two weeks away from high school graduation when his father died in the train wreck. Photograph taken by author.

Because Kroehler lumber yard foreman, Harold Schrader, acted in anticipation of the actual crash, the phone call that he asked the Kroehler operator, Lillian Ory, to make was the first to alert local authorities. After that phone call Ory turned the switchboard over to Rose Staffedlt. Lillian would spend her next hours administering first aid to injured passengers.

Although Ory's phone call for help was undoubtedly the first to be made, there were many others who placed calls. Art Widder, of 252 Fourth Ave., was able to reach Fire Chief Foucek with the news. A Naperville policeman, Martin Prignitz heard the crash from his nearby home. After viewing the tragedy he quickly turned in calls to nearby towns for aid. Such calls quickly had relief coming to the scene from Aurora, Hinsdale, Downers Grove, and other surrounding communities. Mrs. Koppa-Miller and Rosie Hodel also placed calls.

Fire chief Charlie Foucek and Assistant Fire Chief Jack Meluch were among the very first emergency personnel to arrive on the scene. Foucek served two terms as Chief Fire Marshall – the first lasted from 1931 to 1947 and the second from 1951 to 1954. Foucek did not leave the crash site until 11 o'clock the following morning.

Meluch came quickly from his teaching position at the high school just over two blocks away. Police chief, Ed Otterpohl also worked tirelessly both on the 25th and on many days that followed putting together the large amount of paper work required by such a tragedy.

Joe Weigand was another volunteer fire fighter who worked tirelessly at the crash site. Years later Joe would recall entering the last car and seeing people trapped and packed up to the ceiling. Weigand would eventually serve as Naperville's Fire chief from 1954 until 1965.

Photo from the roof of the Kroehler Furniture Company shows a railroad crane used in removal and clean-up efforts. Photograph courtesy of Paul Hinterlong.

After derricks from Morton Park and Aurora had arrived and pulled the imbedded Silver Speed out from car #1376, the movable, functioning cars of the Exposition Flyer were taken back to Chicago. (Note: The train cars that were "totaled" were taken to Eola, Illinois and those that could be repaired were taken to Aurora.) By the time this happened, after 4pm, only a handful of the original passengers were on hand. The conductor of the Exposition Flyer, G.W. Hill, reflected, "I don't have any idea where they (i.e. passengers) all went. They just scattered everywhere."

In fact, some of the passengers hitchhiked on to their hometowns. Some stayed with their injured friends or relatives and waited for others to drive in to assist them. Others waited at the Naperville train station for a new #11 and #39 to transport them home. Still others took the regularly scheduled American Royal to Quincy.

One of those people who hitchhiked was nineteen year old John E. Lundeen. Lundeen was in the sixth coach behind the locomotive on the Exposition Flyer. He had just been discharged from the Great Lakes Naval Training Cener and was returning home to Galesburg. No one was seriously hurt in Lundreen's car. There was, however, a girl who became trapped in the washroom when its door was sprung by the force of the impact. Lundreen and another man helped free the girl.

Mr. and Mrs. Jerry Bulkeley and their children Peter, Christie, and Michael were in the dining car, the fourth car behind the engine of the Exposition Flyer when the crash occurred. The Bulkeleys had just finished their fruit course when they felt the collision. The train bumped over the ties before coming to an abrupt stop. Most of the passengers in the diner were thrown from their chairs as tables overturned and dishes broke.

It took a while for the Bulkeley parents to calm down their children. Then Mr. Bulkeley exited the train and surveyed the scene. When he returned, he decided to keep the children on the train and away from the grotesque images of severed limbs the children would have seen outside. Eventually a relief engine brought the undamaged cars of the Expo back to Chicago where the Bulkeley family boarded another train assembled to take them once again through Naperville and on to their home in Galesburg. The new No. 39 reached Galesburg at 9:05 that night.

The last person who died as a result of injuries incurred in the train wreck was Leona Saylor, a twenty-nine-year-old single government worker returning from Washington, D.C. for a surprise visit to her parents' home in Brunswick, Nebraska. Saylor had notified only her friend Mrs. Dorothy Miller Wilcox of her plans. Miller heard of the accident and when Saylor didn't show up as promised on Thursday night, Dorothy notified first Leona's office in Washington and then Leona's parents.

When she arrived at St. Charles Hospital nurses saw that the initials "ms ¼" had been written across her forehead. This indicated to them that their patient had already been given a shot of a quarter grain of morphine sulfate at the crash site.

Saylor finally succumbed Sunday from injuries including a broken pelvis, bruises, and internal bleeding. Leona's parents had been able to rush to Naperville to be with their daughter before she passed away.

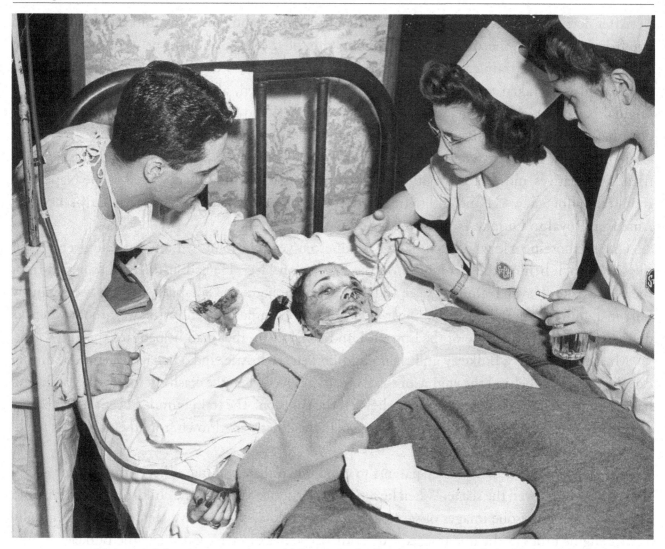

The crash left twenty-nine-year-old Leona Saylor lingering in critical condition. Her parents were able to rush to Naperville and be with their daughter before she died. There is the notation "ms 1/4" on Saylor's forehead. Apparently rescue workers had given Leona a quarter grain of morphine sulfate. Photograph courtesy of Paul Hinterlong.

The victims of the train wreck were not limited to the passengers and crew of the two trains. The sight of the dead and dismembered bodies being removed from the twisted wreckage had striking and indelible effects on rescue workers as well as the many on-lookers. Mrs. Ralph Beardsley, 54, of West Chicago collapsed at the scene as she was watching rescue efforts. She was taken to St. Charles Hospital where doctors treated her for what they determined had been a heart attack.

CHAPTER 5 – NAPERVILLE TRAIN WRECK – WHY?

A Train Went Through a Burial Gate

A train went through a burial gate
A bird broke forth and sang,
And thrilled, and quivered, and shook his throat
Till all the churchyard rang;
And then adjusted his little notes,
And bowed and sang again.
Doubtless, he thought it meet of him
To say good-bye to men.
- Emily Dickinson

It's our nature to try to find explanations and to lay blame for things that break or events that go wrong. And that quest becomes greater the larger, more egregious, and more fatal the catastrophe.

In the case of the Naperville train wreck, there certainly was enough blame to go around. According to the Chicago Daily News of April 26th, the FBI was initially interested in the crash because of the possibility of sabotage. Ultimately, four investigations took place after the April 25th crash.

Burlington railroad officials convened an investigation team on Saturday, April 28th. Burlington officials included division superintendent J.B. Falk and general superintendent S.L. Fee. Photograph courtesy of Paul Hinterlong.

1. The Burlington Railroad quickly assembled an inquiry team that met just two days after the crash. Key members of that panel included A.H. Hanson, H.E Eberle, and G.B. Anderson of the Interstate Commerce Commission; Ralph B. Powers of the Illinois Commerce Commission; J.P. Falk, Burlington division superintendent, and S.E. Fee, Burlington's general superintendent. Testimony at this hearing severely questioned

the actions of Engineer William Blaine. The flagman, the conductor, and the brakeman for the Exposition Flyer, C.W. Norris, George W. Hill, and B.V. Landon all indicated that they observed either a very delayed application of the emergency system or no application whatsoever of that system. Burlington road foreman, W.O. Milar who inspected the train after the crash, stated that he found that the brake valve was in the "service" rather than "emergency" position. Blaine's only support came from the engineer of the Advance Flyer, A.W. Anderson who agreed with Blaine's hospital statement that if his train was trailing more cars, it would have been easier to stop. Blaine was not present at the hearing because he was still in the hospital at the time, but his lawyer, Edward Streit from Aurora, felt that the inquiry was rushed, included only Burlington employees, and did not allow his client to refute any testimony that was given. The DuPage County district attorney, Lee Daniels went further by charging that the Burlington was "rehearsing the evidence". These formal meetings were suspended so that its participants could testify at the grand jury hearings that were to start on Tuesday, May 2nd. On that same May 2nd the Burlington Railroad initiated a series of brake tests in Naperville using the same number of train cars and engine complex all adding up to the weight and brake system similar to that of train #39. The tests ultimately determined that the Exposition Flyer could have been stopped in time if the brakes had been applied at the proper time and in the proper manner by the engineer. Information from this hearing was sent to Washington for further analysis and decisions as to employee culpability.

Deputy Coroner Alan Meyers swears in members of the coroner's investigative panel. From left to right members include: Walter Fredenhagen, Joseph A. Bapst, George Bentz, George A. Erickson, Edward J. Otterpohl, Walter L. Darfer, and Meyers. Photograph from author's collection.

2. The DuPage County Coronor, Paul Isherwood appointed an investigative panel headed by the panel's foreman, W.S. Fredendhagen, owner of the Prince Castle Ice Cream franchise. After the wreck, two of the Prince Castle flatbed trucks had been used to transport bodies to local morgues. Also included on the panel were George Bentz – general contractor; Joseph A. Bapst – jeweler; George A. Erickson – credit manager; Walter Darfler – farmer; and Edward Otterpohl carpenter. It was the recommendation of this coroner's inquest, held at O.J. Beidelman's funeral chapel, that Expositon Flyer engineer, William W. Blaine, be handed over to the grand jury on a manslaughter charge.

3. The Interstate Commerce Commission report – The report was completed on July 30th, 1946 (See appendix for full ICC report and conclusions). It is significant to note that it was not until after the ICC had completed their report that an important causal factor in the wreck may have been discovered. *The Chicago Daily News* reported on August 7th, 1946 that a defective air brake hose was discovered in the second car of the Exposition Flyer. After the crash the car was not returned to service until July 13th. On July 27th railroad mechanics were unable to set the brakes in the emergency position. Upon further examination, mechanics found that part of the air hose had collapsed which prevented the application of the emergency system. C.H. Atkins, a Brotherhood of Locomotive Engineers representative, speculated that "a large blister in the air hose prevented the flow of air behind the blister toward the brake valve." It is difficult to speculate as to whether this defect in the air brake was a cause or result of the Naperville crash.

4. The last investigation was the grand jury investigation. This panel, after lengthy hearings, issued a "no bill" in the case. In other words, they concluded that there was insufficient evidence to convict any one person or group in regard to culpability in the case. The panel, under the guidance of Circuit Judge Win Knoch, did issue eight recommendations in order to prevent future such tragic mishaps:

   a. proper spacing of fast trains using the same right of way.
   b. brake tests on all trains before runs.
   c. use of cars of the same standard equipment and strength on all passenger cars.
   d. equip all passenger trains with radar or other automatic train controls
   e. spacing of safety block signals so as to protect high speed trains.
   f. equipping of all passenger trains with two way radio.
   g. use of Mars oscillating signal lights on the rear of all passenger trains.
   h. requirement that the flagman ride in the rear end and be furnished with more modern warning signals.

Issues that played a part in the Naperville Train Wreck –

- **Burlington Train Schedule:**
Basically, the Burlington train schedule was a mistake waiting to happen. Placing two fast trains on the same track, moving at speeds upwards of 80 to 85 miles per hour, and traveling just three minutes apart was quite simply irresponsible scheduling. The railroad admitted as much when on May 26, 1946 they extended the spacing between the two trains from three minutes to 15 minutes apart.

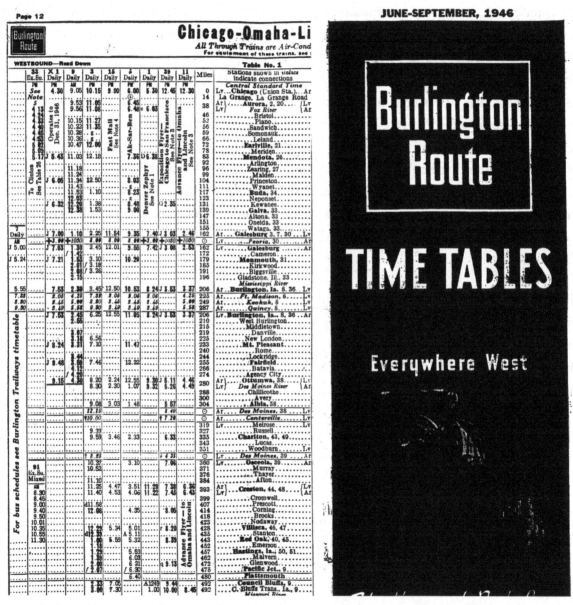

Train schedule...The April 25ᵗʰ, 1946 rail tragedy in Naperville resulted in the implementation of several new preventative safety measures. One of the very first that took place just eight days after the crash involved the change in departure times for the Exposition Flyer (#39) and the Advance Flyer (#11). Departure times between the two trains were separated by fifteen minutes. Burlington schedules courtesy of Jim Christen.

- **The practice of "riding the yellow":**

There was a question as to whether the engineer of the Exposition Flyer applied the emergency brakes in a timely and effective manner. The practice of "riding the yellow" (i.e., slowing down only slightly at the first appearance of a yellow light signal) block signal thinking that the green light would reappear at the next signal standard was a dangerous practice which certainly added to the likelihood of an impending tragedy.

There are two sets of brakes on the pedestal in the cab. One is for the entire *train* and one is for just the *engine* (used mainly in yard work when the engine is hauling just a small number of cars). If the *train* brakes are put into "service" position, the brakes are applied on just the cars in back of the engine. If the *train* brakes are applied full forward in the "emergency" position, then both the engine brakes and the car brakes are engaged. On Sunday, April 29th, a Chicago Tribune reporter interviewed Expo engineer William Blaine. At that time Blaine stated that "the emergency brakes were set and that everything humanly possible had been done to bring the train to a stop". Blaine's attorney, Edward Streit of Aurora would go further and reinforce his client's assertion that he indeed had set both the emergency brakes for the diesel locomotive as well as the air brake that connects with each of the cars. However, the ICC report indicates that after the crash the *train* brakes were found to be only in the service rather than the emergency position. The report makes no mention of the position of the *engine* brakes. At the Burlington inquiry after the crash, the flagman, the conductor, and the brakeman for the Exposition Flyer all testified that they observed either a very delayed application of the emergency system or no application whatsoever of that system.

One of the sailors on the Exposition Flyer was was Motor Machinist's mate, James Getz from Cleveland, Ohio. After the crash Gretz guessed that the train was traveling at about 75 miles an hour as it rounded the bend coming into Naperville. It wasn't until the train had come around the curve that Gretz felt any brakes being applied. After the impact the sailor estimated that the train staggered forward about the length of four telephone poles. It is possible, but not probable that the *train's* emergency brakes were applied, but kicked back into "service" position as a result of the impact of the crash. Later investigative reports do not allow us to make an accurate determination of which brakes were applied, to what extent they were applied, and at what exact moment they were applied. It is interesting to note that because of his injuries, Blaine did not testify at any of the hearings. Unfortunately it took this tragic loss of life before the railroad later added a "flashing yellow" light signal designation, "APPROACH MEDIUM", to advise of a more severe warning of danger ahead. In Naperville they also later added a third light stanchion in the middle of the Naperville curve as a safety aid for trains approaching the town. The Interstate Commerce Commission, heavily influenced by the Naperville train wreck, issued an order in 1947 (effective December 31, 1951) that limited the speeds of trains without an automatic cab signal, automatic train stop, or automatic train control system to 79 miles per hour.

- **Stopping the Advance Flyer on a curve:**

  If the first train had been stopped on a straight-away instead of around a curve, the Exposition Flyer might have been able to see the Advance Flyer ahead and more than likely would have avoided a collision. After the crash, some reporters immediately assumed that a "hotbox" situation was the primary cause of the stoppage of the lead train. However, according to Sherman Grant's own testimony, a "hotbox" does not appear to be the direct motivation for the conductor's action to stop the lead train in this instance. In retrospect, the conductor's decision to stop the train after the Naperville curve was regrettable to say the least.

- **Failure to properly inspect brake equipment**

  The failure of the railroad to more closely inspect the braking equipment may have caused them to overlook a rupture in the brake line that was not found until July 27th, 1946 (Daily News, August 7, 1946).

- **Mixing heavyweight and lightweight consists**

  The placement of heavier cars at the end of the train (two 169,000 pound cars) certainly increased the force pushing into the lighter eleventh car, the Silver Inn dining car (115,800 pounds).

- **Not all cars were equipped with tight interlocking couplers.**

  Only the ninth, tenth, and eleventh lightweight cars had tight interlocking couplers. Since the last two cars did not have such couplers, it appears that the 12th car, the Mississippi, was able to jump out of its connection with both the 13th and 11th cars. Its escape came only after this heavyweight car impacted its damage to the lightweight Silver Inn dining car.

- **Failure of all cars to meet buffing stress standards**

  Few of the consists had center sills that met end-to-end buffing stresses recommended by the Association of American Railroads in 1939 and made standard in 1945. The center sill of the dining car, the Silver Inn, had a cross sectional area of 8.38 square inches. Most cars being built in 1946 had a cross-sectional area of 18 square inches. The Silver Cloud and the Silver Gleam built in 1940 had cross-sectional center sills that were 40% greater than that of the Silver Inn, which was built in 1938. A rear end collision at such speeds is sure to result in a tremendous amount of damage to a car with substandard buffing capability.

- **Exposition Flyer had small load**

  The engineer of the Exposition Flyer felt that he could have stopped his train more easily had it been pulling a heavier load. His train was only pulling 9 cars at the time. A railroad spokesman concurred (Quincy Herald, 4-29-46) with Blaine that a train such as the Exposition Flyer usually accommodated between 12 and 16 coaches. According to a report in the Chicago Daily Tribune (4-27-46) such a diesel engine could handle a maximum load of 22 cars in the summer and 15 cars in the winter.

- **Absence of Engineer Blaine at ICC Investigation**

  The Interstate Commerce Commission's investigation of the accident was impeded by the fact that, due to his hospitalization, the testimony of the engineer of the Exposition Flyer, William W. Blaine, was not included in its report.

- **Mistakes by Flagman James Tangney**

  The miscues of Exposition Flyer's flagman, James Tangney, were negligible but should be mentioned in a list of factors that may have contributed to the extent of the damage incurred. At the time of the crash Tangney was in the wrong car and therefore did not have time to lay down fuses, advance far up the track, or turn on the oscillating light on the rear of car #1376. Still, because of the proximity and speed of the Exposition Flyer, the Naperville curve and the glare from the sun, it is doubtful that any of these omissions significantly affected the ultimate tragic outcome.

EPILOGUE

<u>Grass</u>

Pile the bodies high at Austerlitz and Waterloo.
Shovel them under and let me work—
I am the grass; I cover all.
And pile them high at Gettysburg
And pile them high at Ypres and Verdun.
Shovel them under and let me work.
Two years, ten years, and passengers ask the conductor:
What place is this?
Where are we now?
I am the grass.
Let me work.
—Carl Sandburg

Some days, such as April 25th, 1946 seem long, but the years go by quickly. Yet, the events and people of that tragic spring day are still intimately tied together, even 66 years later.

On the Saturday after the train wreck, Marge Wehrli was married. The celebrant at the ceremony was Father Frederick Stenger. Only two days before, Marge, her sister Calista, and Father Stenger himself were attending to the needs of the victims of the train wreck.

On Sunday Calista received a telegram from the Marine Headquarters informing her that her leave had been shortened and that she was to report immediately back to her base on Parris Island. Calista felt it best that she use the rest of Sunday to recoup from the wedding reception revelry on Saturday night. She traveled back to the base by train on Monday.

When she returned to her command post at Parris Island, South Carolina, she was in for a pleasant surprise. The director of the U.S. Marine Corps Women's Reserve, Colonel Katherine A. Towle, called Calis to tell her that she was being treated to a tour of the White House for her and eight of her friends.

Some time before, Colonel Towle had made a tour of the Parris Island athletic complex. In guiding her commander through the facilities, Calis eventually showed her the swimming complex. The commander mentioned, wishfully, that no one had ever been able to teach her how to swim.

Wehrli said that there was no doubt that she could coach her superior officer to achieve that ability. And, in fact, that's just what she did. Obviously, by this gift of a White House tour, the commander was showing her appreciation.

When Calis and her friends were in the middle of their White House tour, a very unexpected occurrence took place. Suddenly White House guards came forward and with some fanfare, President Truman appeared! When the president saw the marines, he had them line up and spoke to each of them personally. When he came to Wehrli he asked her where she was from. When he heard, "Naperville" given as the reply, he immediately responded, "Oh my, that's where they just had that tragic train wreck." Calis responded, "Yes sir. I was there and helped at the scene for eight hours." The president responded, "You have my thanks and the thanks of a grateful nation."

Father Dunstan's birthday the next day would be very subdued as he recuperated in St. Charles Hospital. After his recovery, Father Velesz would return to his position as teacher of mathematics at Quincy College. Father Velesz also resumed his duties as pastor of St. Benedict Church, an African-American congregation in Quincy, Illinois. Ultimately, Father Dunstan, affectionately known to his friends as Father Dunnie, would serve 63 years as a priest before his death at the age of 89 in 1998.

As unbelievable as it may seem, only two cars from the crash (car #1376 and the Silver Inn diner, both of the Advance Flyer) were damaged to such an extent that they had to be scrapped. The lightweight cars, Silver Gleam and the Silver Cloud, were taken to the Railroad shops in Aurora, Illinois were they were repaired and returned to service. The Silver Gleam resides today at the Atchison Kansas Railroad Museum. The 12th car of the Advance Flyer, the heavyweight "Mississippi", was taken to Aurora and eventually repaired and returned to service as a fluted stainless steel office car "The Round-Up". After 1970 the car was sold to the Canadian National Railroad. It is generally believed that only the Silver Gleam and The Round-Up still survive today from the original consists of the Advance Flyer.

Just six days after the train wreck the Federal Life Insurance company made payment to Mrs. Irene Cherney Miller of a claim on a *Chicago Tribune* travel accident policy on her husband Al Nicholas Miller. A check for $9,750.00 was awarded Mrs. Miller by K. L. Merley, an official of Federal Life Insurance. The payment represented the principal sum of $7,500 plus three annual sums of 10 per cent each. Al Miller took out the policy on January 23, 1942. Premiums were just a little different in those days. At the time of his death Mr. Miller had paid total premiums amounting to only $5.25! (Note: A representative of the Federal Life Insurance Company stated that these types of travel policies offered through newspapers like the Tribune, though quite common at the time, are no longer available). Irene paid off the house with the insurance proceeds and invested the rest in her brother's tool and die shop.

The families of each of the train wreck victims received a settlement of $10,000 from the Burlington Railroad. At the time $10,000 was the limit set by Illinois statute in wrongful death actions and Burlington paid this amount without the need of a suit or a lawyer. Four-year old Ellen Irene Miller and two-year old John Wayne Miller each received a third of the $10,000 in trust which was used for their education.

Readers might remember the Bulkeley family who were traveling on the Exposition Flyer. As a result of the crash, the family was shaken up, but uninjured. Mr. and Mrs. Bulkeley kept their three small children (Peter – 6, Christy – 4, and Michael – 2) on board the Expositon to calm them and to shield them from the horrific scenes they'd see if they had ventured outside.

Christie (now Christy) Bulkeley grew up to be very intelligent and determined. In fact, she became the first woman to be named a chief executive officer of a Gannett owned newspaper. After she left Gannett she earned a Master of Theological Studies degree. Bulkeley died of ovarian cancer on September 13th, 2009. Al Neuharth, founder of *USA Today*, eulogized Christy as "an outstanding journalist and executive".

At the end of 1946, times would be tough for the 800 Kroehler employees and their families. In August of that year Kroehler Furniture Company workers went on a prolonged strike that would last until January, 1947 (Note: This author's father, John Spinner, found employment as a painter during the strike). Yet, for the John and Louise Spinner family, it was all smiles on Sunday, November 4th, 1946. That was day when their new baby, Charles Michael Spinner, in the presence of siblings, godparents (Agnes Spinner and Father Bob Rechenmacher) and assorted relatives, would be baptized by Reverend Frederick R. Stenger at Saints Peter and Paul Church. After the ceremony, there was a reception at the Spinner house at 319 E. 5th Ave across the street from the main office of Kroehler Furniture Manufacturing Company and just a block away from the Loomis Street crossing.

Larry Cena was an eyewitness to the train wreck. He had been recently discharged from military service and was walking to class when he was prevented from crossing the tracks due to the halted Advance Flyer.

At the time, Cena had no particular interest in railroads. However, after college, he found himself working for 38 years with the Santa Fe Railroad. Larry would retire in 1986 at the age of 63 as president and chief executive of the railroad. Cena became Santa Fe's president in 1978 and its chief executive in 1982. Before his retirement he was active in the planning of the merger of the Santa Fe and Southern Pacific Railroads.

Six months after the wreck, there were three injured passengers still undergoing rehabilitation at Aurora's St. Charles Hospital. The three included: 24 year old, Dexter Sexton of Mt. Ayr, Iowa; Mrs. Anna Hovey, 72, of Keokuk, Iowa; and Thomas Chaney, 20 years old, of Council Bluffs, Iowa.

On Monday, November 18th, Dexter Sexton was released from the hospital. Sexton came very close to losing his life due to his many internal injuries, a skull fracture, and broken leg, shoulder, and ribs. He was fortunate to recover and was able to complete his journey home, alone, by train to his home town. Sexton and Chaney became good friends during their hospital recovery period.

Mrs. Hovey and Thomas Chaney were the last two patients from the train wreck to be discharged from the hospital. Anne had suffered two fractured legs in the crash. Her recovery was slowed by several relapses attributable to her advanced age.

Chaney's injuries were numerous and serious. He lost an ear and a leg and he suffered a fractured jaw and a punctured bladder. During his hospital stay he underwent thirteen operations and considerable plastic surgery. Thomas lost 35 pounds during his convalescence.

On December 18, 1946, Thomas Chaney, was released from St. Charles Hospital. Tom's mother, had traveled from Iowa to bring her son home. As Mrs. Chaney saw her son come down the hospital corridor on crutches, she exclaimed, "I don't want another thing for Christmas!"

It is highly likely that this young man came to know the hospital staff quite well. Consequently, during the later stages of his recovery Thomas may have been able to take walks through the halls of the hospital quite freely. It is also quite possible that his curiosity would lead him periodically into the nursery of the maternity ward in order to view the new babies. And, in turn, it is therefore, not out of the realm of possibility that in one of these visits Thomas Chaney may have glanced upon a newborn named Charles Michael Spinner, born to John and Louise Spinner on October 22, 1946. If, indeed he had, I am quite sure that Chaney never dreamt that sixty-five years later, this newborn would write the story of the tragic Naperville train wreck!

On May 5th, 1987, Chuck Spinner received a letter from Nicholas J. DiLorenzo, Sr. Mr. DiLorenzo was the president of MidAmerica Developments, a real estate development company that was just completing a new Naperville subdivision called Knoch Knolls. If the name of the development sounds familiar, it is because the residential community was named after Naperville's own Judge Win Knoch, who, among his many accomplishments, was the judge who presided over the Grand Jury which investigated the potential culpability associated with the Naperville Train wreck of 1946.

Mr. DiLorenzo's letter informed Spinner that his request to have a street named after his grandfather, George Spinner, had been granted. So, now there is a short street, named Spinner Court, containing fourteen houses in the the city of Naperville. The subdivision's brochure mentions that Knoch Knolls is "just 5 miles from the Burlington Railroad Station in Naperville" and that "downtown Chicago is just 30 comfortable air conditioned minutes away".

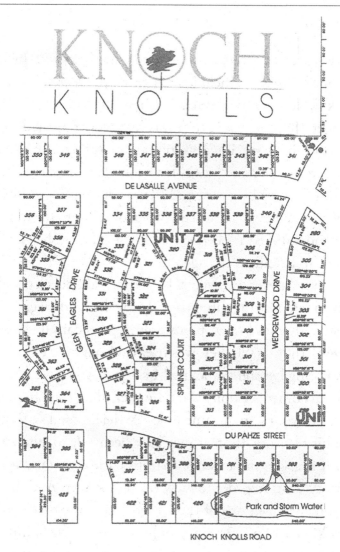

Map of a section of Knoch Knolls development in southern part of Naperville.
"Spinner Court" is indicated. Map courtesy of MidAmerica Federal.

Ron Keller has been the director of the Naperville Community Band since 1966. In 2009 Keller, along with Julie Phend, published "The First 150 Years – A History of the Naperville Municipal Band".

On April 25th, 1946, Ron was a first grader in Miss McDermond's class at Ellsworth School. At approximately 2pm, he was surprised to see his dad standing at his classroom doorway talking with Miss McDermond.

The teacher then motioned for Ron to come to the front of the room. Normally, Ron's route home from school would have him walk west on School Street and then north on Ellsworth Street. He would then take the viaduct under the train tracks to his house. The underpass walkway was right next to the railroad station where passengers from the wreck were already gathering to seek alternate routes home.

Ron Keller's father came to the school that Thursday to drive his son home so as to prevent Ron from seeing the gruesome scenes surrounding the crash site. The alternate route home that day involved driving over the Columbia Street Bridge. As father and son crossed the bridge, Ron noticed the jumbled wreckage on the tracks below and to the west.

Ron remembers asking his dad what had happened; and he also recalls his father's response that one train ran into the back of another train. The youngster wondered why one train just didn't push the other train forward as would inevitably have happened when he played with his Lionel train set!

☆ ☆ ☆

What Happened To:

Harold Schrader

Sixty three years after the crash, in the summer of 2009, this author interviewed ninety-eight year old **Harold Schrader**, who, at the time, was one of only two living eye witnesses to the crash.

Harold lived a very active life both before and after the train wreck of 1946. Schrader was a charter member of the Naperville Municipal Band and played the baritone sax for the group for sixty one years! He was very involved as an adult Boy Scout leader. Harold enjoyed wood working, and for a number of Christmases he dressed up as Barney the Elf and sat in a downtown Naperville store window creating wooden toys.

In 2008 Harold and his wife Mary celebrated their seventy-sixth wedding anniversary! That same year the Naperville Heritage Society inducted the couple into its Heritage Hall of Honors.

Harold's mind was still sharp as a tack up to his death on March 13, 2011 at the age of ninety-nine!

Harold Schrader, Kroehler yard foreman and eye witness to wreck, opens cards on his 98th birthday. Photograph taken by Carol Lee Schrader Cole.

Raymond "Jake" Jaeger,

Contact was also made with Raymond "Skip" Jaeger Jr. whose father miraculously survived the crash as a passenger in car #1376. Unfortunately, Skip's dad, eighty-eight year old **Raymond "Jake" Jaeger**, had died on January 26, 2008, just months before Spinner's call. The junior Jaeger had been given the nickname "Skip" by his father during the war. In his letters home, his father would always ask how his little "Skipper" was doing. The nickname stuck.

After the train wreck Raymond worked forty-one years for the Leopold Desk Company in Burlington, Iowa until his retirement in 1981. The interests of this avid Chicago Cubs fan included duck hunting, fishing in the Mississippi River, and gardening. Jaeger was preceded in death by his wife Helen Bragg Jaeger. The Jaegers were married for 65 years, had seven children, ten grandchildren and, at the time of Jake's death, sixteen great grandchildren along with two great great grandchildren.

Ultimately, Spinner was able to arrange a conference call between Calista Wehrli and Raymond

Jaeger Jr., who at that time, was able to express his great appreciation for the help Calis had given his father back on April 25, 1946.

Wesley "Blaine" Overman

Among the many interviews the author had with people involved with the tragedy, the situation involving contact with **Wesley Overman** stands out. Wesley had been just slightly injured in the wreck and helped other passengers out of their overturned car, the Silver Cloud. Over six decades later, Spinner made contact by phone with Overman at his farm in Caldwell, Idaho. When he called at the arranged time, Overman's daughter apologized and said that her eighty-eight year old father was still out pruning vines in the family's 3 acre table grape vineyard. She assured the author that her dad would be anxious to call and talk about the wreck when he came back to the house.

During the ensuing interview Mr. Overman stated that he was born in Beloit, Kansas but that because of the "Dust Bowl" his family moved out to Idaho in 1936. On April 25th, 1946 he was on furlough from Fort Campbell, Kentucky, and was taking the train back home to visit his folks. Blaine received his discharge from the army not long after the train wreck. He then returned to his home in Caldwell where he got married in 1950. He and his wife Suzanne raised three daughters and one son. Overman then worked 46 years for J.R. Simplot whom he knew personally. He first worked as a foreman for the Richardson/J.R. Simplot Feedlot and then drove a truck and hauled potatoes, grain, fertilizer, sand, etc. for the company. J.R. Simplot's agricultural organization was formed in 1948 and is credited with creating the first commercial frozen french fry. In 1967 when Ray Kroc contracted with Simplot to supply french fries for the McDonald chain, Simplot's financial success was assured. Since Overman's retirement from the Simplot company he has taken over a dozen fishing trips to Alaska. The Overman's still live on the farm that they purchased in 1961.

Anna Koppa-Miller.

Anna Koppa-Miller lived in the house closest to the train wreck. Her kitchen served as a first aid station after the crash.

The Koppa-Miller house is noteworthy in Naperville history even without its participation in the 1946 tragedy. Anna's husband, Arthur, built the striking stone house in 1915 using fieldstone, river rock, and boulders gathered from the area. Because of the proximity of the train tracks, Arthur could usually find some hobos to help him move some of the larger rocks into place. These transient men knew that their efforts would always be rewarded with a great meal from Anna's kitchen.

After the train wreck Anna's mind was never quite the same. It was thought that she suffered from post-traumatic stress syndrome. Over the years she also developed arteriosclerosis and died at Edwards Hospital on January 3rd, 1958.

Royal Lauing

In April of 1946 Anna and Arthur's daughter, Marcianna, was engaged to **Royal Lauing**. Lauing was one of the many Naperville citizens who left their work to help at the crash site. Mr. Lauing died June 28, 2007. Royal and Marcianna had two children, Carolyn and Daniel.

Wallace "William" Blaine

The engineer of the Exposition Flyer, Wallace "William" Blaine, a resident of Galesburg, Illinois lived ten years after the train crash. Blaine would not return to work after the wreck. William was hospitalized on January 8th, 1956 and died five days later. He was 78 years old.

At his death Blaine was survived by his wife, Irma (Cunningham) Blaine to whom he had been married 49 years. William and Irma had three sons, Maurice C, Donald F, and Gerald E. At the time of his death, the couple had three grandsons. Blaine's three brothers preceded him in death.

William Blaine's tombstone in Linwood Cemetery, Galesburg, Illinois, gives no indication that he was the engineer of the ill fated Exposition Flyer just 10 years earlier. Photograph taken by Travis Huffman.

Thomas Chaney

After his recovery from his serious injuries suffered in the wreck, Thomas Chaney received a business degree from Omaha's Creighton University and set out in 1949 as an associate manager of an insurance agency. In addition to his insurance work Chaney ran a cleaning plant from 1949 to 1954.

It was at this point that Chaney would encounter a situation of a different nature, but almost as challenging as the physical troubles he had experienced earlier. In 1955 he and an acquaintance, Robert Willis, were accused of involvement in the robberies of a service station and a liquor store. Willis was driving Chaney's car during the service station robbery and he was sentenced to eight years in prison. Thomas' case was eventually dismissed after four years of litigation and court delays due to periods of time when illnesses caused Chaney to be hospitalized.

Having his court troubles behind him, Chaney opened up Tom

1957 picture of Tom Chaney courtesy of the Pottawatamie County Geneological Society.

Chaney Cleaners and Laundry in 1957. From 1962 to 1970 Thomas was a vending machine operator and in 1972 he ran unsuccessfully for Pottawattamie County Board of Supervisors.

Thomas Chaney died on January 12, 1976 at the age of 50. His obituary stated that he was survived by a son, Thomas Jr., who at the time was serving in the U.S. Navy.

Calista Wehrli

After the train wreck **Calista Wehrli** finished her stint with the U.S. Marines. She then received a bachelor's degree in education from Iowa State Teachers College and a master's degree in physical education from UCLA.

Calista taught a total of ten years at Pasadena College, SanFrancisco State University, and the University of California, Berkley. She then had a stellar eighteen year career as a physical education teacher at Ontario High School in Ontario, California. Her influence there is demonstrated by the fact that the high school's swimming facilities are named after her.

Calista was one of thirteen Wehrli children; she never married and lived to the age of 85. She died peacefully on September 6, 2010. The author was honored to have been able to interview Calis several times for this work.

In November, 2009, author Chuck Spinner interviewed eighty-four-year-old
Calista Wehrli. As a young marine reservist sixty-three years earlier, Calis spent
eight hours helping at the crash site. Photograph taken by Janet Wehrli.

Rosie Hodel

Fiesty, outspoken **Rosie Hodel** worked for a total of 45 years for two of Naperville's most important employers of the period. She worked for twenty seven years at Kroehlers and then eighteen years at the Moser Lumber Company.

Years after the crash Rosie Hodel would reflect that "Naperville in those days was a sleepy little farm town. The most exciting thing was when the beach opened or the band concerts. Of course, when you were 18 it was pretty exciting to sneak beers." In one of her last interviews before she died Rosie reflected "That was some wreck! I wonder how many people who live in Naperville now know the wreck happened?"

Arnie Hodel

One of her brothers, **Arnie Hodel**, helped as a volunteer fire fighter at the crash scene. Arnie worked for the Naperville Fire Department for forty years before his retirement. He was appointed full time engineer in 1959, assistant chief in 1962, and chief in 1964. Arnie and his wife retired to Fairview, Arkansas to relax and to fish. Fairview at the time did not have a fire department or a fire chief. It has both now.

Rose and Arnie were two of eight Hodel children. Rosie Hodel never married. She passed away at the age of eighty-four on April 29, 2009.

APPENDIX

NAPERVILLE, ILLINOIS TRAIN WRECK OF APRIL 25, 1946 - FATALITIES

Age of victims noted in parenthesis

1. Abbott, Arthur (49)
2. Aman, Dorothy Lee (22)
3. Anderson, August H. (68)
4. Boon, Delbert (21)
5. Brown, Ralph Vance (47)
6. Bentler, Joe(73)
7. Carr, Daniel Nathaniel (51)
8. Chamberlain, Charles (45)
9. Collins, Charlotte (71)
10. Conner, Eugene Everett (35)
11. Craft, Marian Johanna Brickman (25)
12. Crayton, Curtis H.(45)
13. Dickhut, Kenneth W. (30)
14. Farley, Mary Alberta (42)
15. Flotkoetter, Kay Loomis(22)
16. Howard, Richard E. (19)
17. King, Elves Alexander (69)
18. Lane, Albert J. (56)
19. Langen, Mary (49)
20. Lawrence, Margaret (71)
21. Lawrence, Matthew (80)
22. Lett Jr., Elza (27)
23. Long, Harry W. (21)
24. Mennen, Mayme (69)
25. Miller, Al N. (37)
26. Moos, Leo P. (66)
27. Moos, Rosa (57)
28. Ralston, John Nicholas (45)
29. Robinson, Fred (62)
30. Rohr, Elizabeth (72)
31. Rohr, Abraham (75)
32. Saylor, Leona (29)
33. Schuetz, Emma (64)
34. Sherwood, E. Read (35)
35. Sromovsky, Sophie Vehosty (29)
36. Stimpson, Howard Clinton (20)
37. Takashima, Lucy (23)
38. Voss, Bernard H. (28)
39. Whitehead Eleanor (35)
40. Whitehead, Russell L. (34)
41. Wiley, Maralyn (28)
42. Wiley, Randy M. (1)
43. Wiley, Terry L. (3)
44. Wilson, Florence (45)
45. Yarbrough, Clifford (58)

List of Injured Receiving Hospital Treatment as a Result of Naperville Train Wreck

(listed as recorded from accumulated news accounts of crash - at least twenty others received basic first aid at Aurora hospitals and released without being recorded)

1. Blaine, William W., 68, Galesburg, Ill., engineer on Exposition Flyer; concussion.
2. Braxton, Ellis, 38, Negro, Chicago, Ill., bruises.
3. Brown, Ernest, 43; Negro, Chicago, Ill., bruises.
4. Butler, Charles W., 50, Negro cook, Chicago, Ill., burns and lacerations.
5. Carter, Vernon, 42, Negro, waiter, Chicago, Ill., bruises, head injuries.
6. Chamberlain, Charles, 45, Negro, waiter, Chicago, Ill., severe injuries.
7. Chaney, Thomas, 20, Council Bluffs, Iowa, merchant seaman, fractured pelvis, severed leg and ear, fractured jaw, punctured bladder.
8. Cook, Mrs. Irene Whitehouse, 20, Cohoes, N.Y., condition serious.
9. Cooper, Mattie, 82, Hutsonville, Ill., lacerations of face and knee.
10. Donegan, Don, 48, Negro cook, Chicago, Ill., shoulder and arm burns and lacerations.
11. Drennan, C.O., Aurora, Illinois.
11. Dugen, Mrs. Douglas, Carthage, Illinois.
11. Evjen, Mrs. John O., Carthage, Ill., a widow, broken leg and arm, concussion, scalp wound, bruises.
12. Faber, Mr. and Mrs. Henry J., 28 & 27, Keokuk, Iowa, bruises and lacerations, stomach and back injuries.
13. Greenbaum, Sol, 27, St. Louis, Missouri, sprained ankle.
14. Henne, Mrs. Clara, housewife, Omaha, Nebraska, bruises.
15. Hovey, Mrs. Anne, 72, Keokuk, Iowa, fractured legs.
16. Jaeger, Pvt. Raymond, 21, Burlington, Iowa, wounded Marine, bruises.
17. Kyer, Ruth H., Hannibal, Missouri, fractured shoulder, head injuries
18. McBride, William E., 26, Negro waiter, burns and lacerations.
19. Melton, William A., condition critical, head and internal injuries.
20. McIntosh, John, 43, orange grower of San Diego, CA., back and leg injuries.
21. McCloud, Julius, Negro, waiter on Exposition Flyer, Gary, Indiana, back and chest injuries.
22. Peters, Miss Ruth, 32, Washington, D.C., fractured legs, shock, critical.
23. Ringold, Henry E., Scarsdale, New York, cuts on face and hand.
24. Sexton, Dexter A. Jr., 26, Mount Ayr, Iowa, lacerations, critical.
25. Sromovsky, Sgt. John S., 29, Plymouth, Pa., pelvic injuries, condition good.
26. Sumpter, Harrison, 38, Negro waiter, Chicago, Ill., burns and lacerations
27. Velesz, Rev. Dunston, member of faculty of St. Francis College, Quincy, Ill., fractured right leg, minor injuries.
28. Whitehouse, Mrs. Florence, 46, Cohoes, NY, leg amputation, shock, condition critical.

In 2010 Naperville's DuPage Children's Museum was selected by Nickelodeon Parents Picks as Best Chicago Museum and in 2006 Crain's Chicago Business ranked it as one of the top ten Chicagoland Cultural Attractions. The museum is located within easy walking distance of Naperville's train station. The three story facility has a section dedicated to the importance of the railroad to Naperville's history. Photograph taken by author.

THE NAPERVILLE POLICE REPORT AND
THE INTERSATE COMMERCE COMMISSION REPORT

Department of Police

CITY OF NAPERVILLE
NAPERVILLE, ILLINOIS

April 25, 1946

Mr. Edward C. Otterpohl, as per your request I hereby submit the following report concerning the train wreck on the C.B.& Q. R.R. at the Loomis Street crossing on above date.

I was at the Police Station when I heard the sound of the crash. A telephone call followed about one minute later and I proceeded to the scene immediately arriving there about 1:08 P.M.

Officer L. Gieske arrived about the same time. I instructed him to call for ambulances, doctors, and other police departments for help, and then proceeded to help remove the dead and injured from the wreckage on the south side of the right-of-way. As more help arrived I went to the North side of the wreckage to see what was being done there. I found that employees of Kroehler Mfg. Company were well organized in a rescue team and were taking care of the dead and injured.

My next move was to locate and take statements from the crews of each train. I succeeded in finding only a few to question. The names and statements are as follows:

(Conductor J. Aue, Rockford, Ill., in charge of Train
No. 11 the Advance Flyer.)
Diesel No. 9920   B & A   13 car train left Chicago
12:35 P.M. Westbond.
Some members of crew heard something fly out from under one of the coaches and they stopped to investigate.
Stopped at 1:03 P.M., was hit by train No. 39 about one and one-half minutes later. Also stated that his flagman J. Tangney was out about one minute.
Other members of the crew were:
         Engineer - A.W. Anderson - Galesburg, Ill.
         Brakeman - Sherm Grant - Chicago, Ill. CRAYTON - JUMPED + DIED
         Fireman - Could not locate.
         Flagman - J. Tangney - Aurora, Ill.

Conductor Geo. Hill, 805 S. 8th, Burlington, Iowa, in charge of Train No. 39 (Exposition Flyer)
                                      (Nebraska Special)
Diesel No. 9910   A & B.   9 car train left Chicago
12:35 P.M. Westbound.

Conductor Hill stated he did not notice an application of brakes on his train prior to the crash. Other members of the crew are:

Engineer - W.G. Blaine - Galesburg, Ill.
(Fireman - Craydon - no address given,   )
(jumped from the locomotive some distance   )
(east of Loomis St., crossing before the   )
(crash.   )
Brakeman - C. W. Norris,- Burlington, Iowa.
Flagman - B. V. Landon - Galesburg, Ill.

By that time most of the dead and injured had been removed, so I inspected the coaches of train No. 39 and found several passengers with minor injuries. They were:

Kay Holland, 901 West Carrol, McComb, Ill.
Age 13. (Abdomen)

Loyd Thurston, Osceola, Iowa. Age 65. Nose injury.

Ellis Braxton, 3739 S. Wabash. Cuts on eye, nose, head.

Chas. J. Cantwell, 617 K St., Sacramento, Calif. Knee injury.

Freddie Stanley, Camp Beal, Calif., arm injury.

Robert Lapson, 2065 E. 8th, Brooklyn, N.Y. Nose injury.

After talking to the Conductors of both trains and judging from the position of the wreckage, it appeared to me that train No. 39 telescoped into the rear chair car of train No. 11 passing about two-thirds of the way through the car. The second car from rear of train No. 11 was the chair coach Mississippi which remained upright. The third car from rear evidently was the diner which was demolished. The fourth car from the rear of No. 11 apparently was chair car No. 4710 which was tipped over. Next car in line was Silver Gleam No. 4703 which remained upright. Other cars of No. 11 had been moved some distance away by this time.

Most of the casualties were in the rear chair car and in the dining car of train No. 11.

Department of Police

OLIVER J. BEIDELMAN FUNERAL HOME

CITY OF NAPERVILLE
NAPERVILLE, ILLINOIS

#1..John M. Ralston, OJB
620 Laurel Ave
Des Plaines, Ill,

#2..Mrs. Elizabeth Rohr, OJB
wife #37
Chicago, Ill.

#3..A. H. Anderson, OJB ✓
3403 Laura
Lincoln, Nebr.

#4..Mrs. Rose Moose, OJB ✓
516 Seventh St.,
Moorehead, Minn.

#5..Leo P. Moos, OJB ✓
516 Seventh St.,
Moorehead, Minn.

#6..Mary Farley, OJB ✓
2236 Jones St.,
Omaha, Nebr.

#7..Danice N. Carr, OJB ✓
2059 W. Roosevelt
Chicago, Ill.

#8..Albert J. Lane, OJB ✓
7519 N. Claremont
Chicago, Ill.

#9..E. Read Sherwood, OJB ✓
18 S. Michigan
Chicago, Ill.

#10.R. L. Whitehead, OJB
19 Richmond
Weymouth, Mass.

#11.Mrs. Margaret Lawrence, OJB ✓
1002 S. Tenth
Escanaba, Mich.

#12.Mrs. Mary Langen, OJB ✓
2515 Chesnut St.
Quincy, Ill.

#13,Clifford Yarbrough ✓
504 N. Eighth St.

#14..Emily Schuetz, OJB
Lombard, Ill

#15..Harry W. Long, OJB ✓
Burlington, Ia.

#16..Everett E. Connor, OJB ✓
310 Penn Ave
South Bend, Ind.

#17..Richard Joe Bentler, OJB ✓
W. Point, Ia.

#18..Dorthy Lee Aman, OJB ✓
2919 Pratt,
Omana

#19..Richard E. Howard, OJB ✓
Mich.

#20..Elsa Lett Jr. ARB ✓
Kenora, W. Va.

#21..Fred Robinson, ARB
Council Bluffs, Ia.

#22..Terry Lee Wiley, 4 yrs, AR-OJB ✓

#23..Ronald Wiley 2 yrs ✓
6324 S. LaVergne
Chicago, Ill

#24..Mrs. Marian Crafts, ARB ✓
1821 State St.
Quincy, Ill

#25..Mrs. Kay Flatkoetter, ARB ✓
Quincy, Ill

#26..Ralph Brown, ARB
6442 Evans Ave.
Colored, Chicago

#27..E. A. King, ARB ✓

Department of Police

CITY OF NAPERVILLE
NAPERVILLE, ILLINOIS

#28..Al Miller, ARB
    4827 Oakdale
    Chicago

#29..Mrs. Elenor Whitehead, ARB ✓
    Weymouth, Mass.

#30..Mrs. Charlotte Collins, ARB ✓ (2)
    Hannibal, Mo.

#31..Bernard Voss, Navy, ARB ✓
    RFD #2, N. 12th St.
    Quincy, Ill.

#32..Kenneth Dickhut, ARB ✓
    USA, Quincy

#33.. *Howard Stimpson*
    Great Lakes,

#34..Mrs. Pl L. (Mayme) Mennen, BF ✓
    1314 Jefferson St.
    Burlington, Ia.

#35..Mrs. Marlyn Wiley, BF-OJE ✓
    6324 S. La Verne
    Chicago,

#36..Mrs. Florence Wilson, BF ✓
    State College, Pa.

#37..Abraham Rohr, BF
    5444 Potomac -
    Chicago

DINING CAR STEWARD

#38..Arthur Abbott, Stewart, BF
    Berwyn, Ill.

104

Department of Police

CITY OF NAPERVILLE
NAPERVILLE, ILLINOIS

Oliver J. Beidelman Funeral Home: *#267*

# 1 Envelope John M. Ralston 620 Laurel Ave., Desplaines, Illinois	#10 Env. R. L. Whitehead 19 Richmond Weymouth, Mass.
#2 "	#11 "
#3 " A. H. Andersen 3403 Laura, Lincoln, Neb.	#12 " Mrs. C. S. Langen 2515 Chestnut St., Quincy, Illinois
#4 " '	#13 " Clifford Yarbrough 504 N. 8th St., Vandalia, Ill.
#5 " Leo P. Moos 516 Seventh St., Moorehead, Minn.	#14
#6 " *MARY JONES SMALL BLACK PURSE.* *2236 JONES Street* *OMAHA NEBRASKA.*	#15 Harry W. Long, Burlington, Iowa
	#16 Everett E. Conner 310 Penn Ave., South Bend, Ind.
#7 " Danice N. Carr 2059 W. Roosevelt Rd., Chicago, Illinois	#17 Joe ~~Bentler~~ W. Point, Iowa
#8 " Albert J. Lane 410 N. Michigan Ave., Chicago, Illinois	#18
#9 " E. Read Sherwood 18 S. Michigan Ave., Chicago, Illinois (Stevens Hotel)	#19 Richard E. ~~Howard~~ 753-31-322 (Tattoo)

Six women unidentified   *22}*
23} children
24—

Arthur Beidelman Funeral Home

#20 Elsa Lett Jr. Kenova, W. Va. *21* Fred Robinson Council Bluff, Iowa	R. V. Brown Chicago, Illinois L. N. Millen, Chicago, Ill.
22 A. J. Wiley ----Mother and two small sons Chicago, Illinois	
#25 Mrs. K. Flotkoetten	3/ E. H. Voss -- Sailor
	3. Kenneth Dickhut

#34 Mayme Mennen (Burlington Iowa) W. Jefferson

#37 Abraham Rohr — 5444 Potomac ave. Chicago

#35 Maralyne Wiley — 6324 S. La Vergne — Chicago.

Aurther R Abbott — 3420 Grove ave — Berwyn Ill.

Dining car Steward.

#36 Florence Wilson

#27 King

OLIVER J. BEIDELMAN

Licensed Embalmer

FURNITURE AND UNDERTAKING

NAPERVILLE, ILLINOIS

1 ✓
    Mrs. Mary Langen ✓
    2515 Chestnut St.
    Quincy, Ill

14
    Emily Schutz ✓
    Lombard, Illinois

11
    Mrs. Margaret Lawrence — ✓
    1002 S. 10th
    Escanaba, Michigan

2
    Mrs. Elizabeth Rohr ✓
    Chicago, Illinois

36 Florence Wilson
   Still college Pa.

34 Mrs P L Swenson
   Banking Com Div

#6 Mary A Farley ✓
   Omaha Nebraska

#30 Mrs Charlotte Collins
    Hannable Missouri

#32 Kenneth Dickhart
    Quincy Ill.

#7 Daniel N Carr
   Chicago

Department of Police

CITY OF NAPERVILLE
NAPERVILLE, ILLINOIS

Crafts, Marian J.   1821 State St.   Quincy, Illinois   #24

107

List of Injured at St. Charles Hospital.

BLAINE,WM.WALLACE   68,1479 Summit St. Galesburg —
Braxton,Ellis   38,3739 South Wabash, Chi —
Brown,Ernest   43,2243 Forrestville Ave. Chi —
Chaney,Thomas   20,Route 3 Council Bluff,Iowa,Seaman —
Cook,Irene Whitehouse,20 161 Manor Ave. Cohoes,N.Y. —
Cooper,Mattie,   82, Hutsonville,Ill. —
Carter,Vernon   42,   5842 Michigan Ave. Chi — *Employee - Property ok money returned ok*
~~Eugen, Mrs.Douglas~~   Carthage,Ill *MRS. JOHN O. EVGEN — money returned ok*
Faber, Mrs. Henry J. 28, 28 South 11th St. Keokuk,Ia. — } *money + valuables returned ok.*
Faber, Henry   27   Same —
Greehbaum,Sol   27   4914 LaClede St. St.Louis Mo. —
Henne,Mrs.Clara   1111 South 49th Ave. Omaha,Neb. — *Home*
Hovey,Mrs.Anne   Keokuk, Ia. — *money + valuables returned ok.*
Jaeger,Pvt.Ramond,   26 Navy Hospital, Great Lakes,Ill (Burlington,Ia) —
Kyer,Ruth   Hannibal,Mo. — *money + valuable returned ok*
McCloud,Julius,   Gary , Ind. —
McIntosh,John   43   San Diego,Calif — *to be released from Hospital 4/28/4*
Melton, W.A.   *533 - 46 St Chgo —*
Saylor,Leana *LEONA*   1526 17th St.Washington D.C.27 > *Expected to die 4/2*
Sexton,Dexter A.Jr. 23   Mt.Ayr,Ia. —
Sromovshy,John A 29 .   Ft.Robinson,Neb. — *taken to Fort Sheridan by army*
Velesz,Rev.Duston   St.Francis College, Quincy,Ill —

                          DEAD.....St. Charles Hospital — *Coronion*
39 Boon,Delbert,175 W.Jackson Chi.   Home Lorraine,Mo.
40 Chamberlain,Chas   45 3229 Rose Ave   Chi. (waiter) — *Healthy*
41 Crayton,G.N.(FIREMAN H32) 575 Monmouth, Galesburg,Ill
42 Lawrence,Matt   Escanaba,Mich.
43 Sromovsky, Sophie 29 Ft.Robinson,Neb. — *Polyider —*
44 *Takashima (Miss Fumy) Or money nurse body at Healy*
                          List of Injured at Copley Hospital

Butler,Charles William   50 5934 South Parkway Chi, (Negro) —
Donegan,   Don   46 4738 St.Lawrence   Chi   " —
McBride,William   26 1542 Calumet   Chi   " —
Peters,Miss Ruth   47 Washington,D.C.   *White* —
Whitehouse,Mrs.Florence   46 161 Manor Ave.Cahoe,N.Y. (White) —
Sumpter,Harrison   38 3743 Indiana Ave. Chi   (Negro) —

Slightly Injured

Robert Japson 2065 E. 8th nose injury Brooklyn New York
Charles Cantwell 617 K St Knee injuries Sacramento California
Freddy Stanley company Beal California face injury
Fayld Thurston Osceola Iowa nose injury
Ellis Braxton 3739 S Wabash cut on eye Chicago Porter

108

Mrs. Elizabeth Rohr - large suit case
Mrs. F.L. Mennen - broken suit case - 2 purses
Mrs. E.B. Schmitz - suit case - paper envelope - purse
M/Sgt. J.A. Sromovsky - large suit case - shaving kit
Leona B. Sayler - suit case - purse *Dead.*
Edward R. Sherwood - brief case - paper envelope - *Rush*
Irene B. Whitehouse - suit case - *Dr. Whitehead*
~~Mrs. Ann Hovey - suit case - purse~~
~~Bernard H. Voss - cardboard box~~ *Rush*
~~Mrs. Edith Faber - suit case - purse~~
Daniel N. Carr - broken suit case *Rush*
C.W. Butler - suit case - shaving kit
L. Wilson - hand bag *Rush*
~~Vernon Carter - suit - overcoat - wallett~~
Howard C. Stimpson - suit case *Rush*
~~Henry Faber - shaving kit~~
Richard E. Howard - suit case *Rush*
~~Lucy Takashima - card board box containing broken suit case - purse~~ *Rush*
Dora Kyer - wine colored robe and clothes
~~Mrs. J.O. Evjen - purse~~
Irene Cook - purse - *Dr. Whitehead*
~~Ruth Kyer or Louise Kyer - purse~~
Mrs. William Aman - purse - paper envelope - package *Rush*
Mrs. Florence Wilson - purse *Rush*
Harry W. Long - broken suit case *Rush*
~~Rev. Father Dunstan Velasz - brief case - will pick up~~
Ralp Brown - paper envelope *Rush*
Al Miller - paper envelope - wallett *Rush*
~~Elsa Lett Jr. - paper envelope~~ *Rush*
Fred Robinson - paper envelope *Rush*
Chas. Chamberlain - wallett *Rush*
Geo. Whitney - wallett
John Ralston - paper envelope *Rush*
~~Eleanor Whitehead - paper envelope~~ *Rush*
Arthur Abbott - paper envelope *Rush*
Leo Moos - paper envelope ✓
R. L. Whitehead - paper envelope - suit case *Rush*

Department of Police

CITY OF NAPERVILLE
NAPERVILLE, ILLINOIS

Received the following unidentified property

One black plastic draw string purse, empty when found, now contains 23¢.

One folding Kodak Camera, film #116.

One leather key case, containing 2 Plymouth keys.

One gold colored lapel pin, USNR

One black glossy cloth coin purse containing $1.46.

One black leather coin purse containing $3.

One man's large gold diamond ring with square white gold setting

One gold band wedding ring, initialed KME to ERL, 7918-36.

2-$1 bills.

One yellow gold pearl ear ring.

One heart shaped necklace with a cross.

$1.54 in change.

One glass case containing nose piece, Charles W. Collins
                                      615 No. Section
                                      Hannnibal, Mo.

4 loose cigarette lighters, 1 Dunhill, 1 Ronson, and 2 Berkeley lighters.

1 inkograph pen

1 Eversharp life time pencil

1 Osborne mechanical pencil

1 yellow gold eye glass frame

1 dress ornament, gold spider

1 turquoise dress ornament

1 bird design dress ornament

1 Virgin Mary necklace

page 2

1 black lady's purse with gold ball fastener, containing, rabbit foot on chain, 1-$2.50 gold piece, 2-$10 bills, 1-$5 bill, 3-$1 bills.

1 coin purse containing, 3 keys on chain with identification tag Pa, 1945 state license #6GK52, one pair ear rings with large gold bars and $12.75 in cash.

1 black leather flat purse containing, one pair black cloth gloves, one white coint purse, one blue butterfly pin, one blue center gold pin, one pearl choker, one amber choker with three stones, one deck small playing cards and one black coin purse containing 15-$1 bills and $1.98 in change.

1 man's brown leather toilet kit.

One new gabardine top coat, labeled Straus Quality Clothes, Fargo and Valley City, containing 1 pair black leather gloves and 7 La-Palina DeLuxe cigars in pocket. Man's.

One gabardine top coat, labeled Botany, Henry C. Lytton & Sons, one package Tums in pocket.

One light brown tweed top coat, labeled Henry C. Lytton & Sons.

One brown top coat man's labeled Harvey Bros, pocket contained key for Paxton Hotel, Paxton Neb. room 1134, bank book for Bank of Chadron, Chadron, Neb.

3 pairs brown pants and 2 new neck ties. Tom Chaney written on inside of one pair.

One tan rain coat labeled Belster.

One lady's light blue coat, labeled Davids Cleveland, one pair earrings in pocket.

One lady's brown coat, labeled Lazaras, Wilkesbarre, Pa.

One dark blue man's overcoat labeled, Luxora

One old style tobacco pouch containing 15¢.

Received signed _R. L. Carroll_

Title _____

Address _Chicago_

Page 2

Department of Police

CITY OF NAPERVILLE
NAPERVILLE, ILLINOIS

Received the following personal property and effects of

Russell L. Whitehead, 1 black billfold containing $54 in currency and $1.62 in change., 1 Clinton wrist watch gold color with brown leather band.

Fred Robinson
124 Bluff St.
Council Bluffs, Ia.
SS 480-09-3693

Total cash $290.84, 1 diamond ring large square diamond setting, 1-$2 bill, 1-$1 bill and one old style $10 bill, one $2.50 gold piece, one Sussex stainless steel wrist watch with stainls steel band, 12 keys on ring with identification tag #3887, Council Bluffs Savings Bank, Council Bluffs, Ia., one pearl handled pocket knife and one gold tie clasp.

Al N. Miller

One pair eye glasses, $1.72 in change, 5 loose keys, one false gold pocket knife.

Dr. L. P. Moos

$1 in change, this money was found by Sgt. Rickert after the Coroner had made his search.

Ralph Brown
no address
CB&Q employee

One CB&Q payroll check amount of $47.45, one black billfold containing $1.34 in change.

John N. Ralston
690 Laurel Ave.
Des Plaines, Ill.
SS 339-09-5589

One Waterman gold capped pen and pencil set, one old square gold wrist watch Waltham, keys with identification tag # E-30991 Traverlers Ins Co/ Hartford, Conn., $130 in currency and $1.03 in change, 1 rosary with red beads, 1 tie clasp initialed JNR. This was also found later by Sgt. Rickert after Coroner had completed his search.

E. R. Sherwood

One blue cloth money belt containing 5-$10 bills. This was also found later by Sgt. Rickert.

Peter Mennen

One brown billfold containing 1-$5 bill, one black folder containing 3-$10 American Express Traverler Cheques made out to Mary Mennen, one Farmers & Merchants Savings Bank deposit book showing $1000 deposited in the name of Mary Mennen, one black cloth coin purs containing $3.36.

Mrs. Hene

One folder containing papers and pair eye glasses.

Mrs. H K. Wilson

One leather black draw sting purse containing one gold compact, one pair plastic rimmed eye glasses, 4-3¢ and 3-1¢ postage stamps.

R L S Pagel

Department of Police

page 2

L. Wilson   One brown canvas bag containing army clothing.

E. R. Sherwood   One black brief case, contents not checked.
8 So. Michigan
Chicago, Ill.

Harry W. Long   One torn brown and cream striped bag, zipper top,
2319 Sunnyside   contents not checked.
Burlington, Ia.

Mrs. Elizabeth Rohn   One large airplane type bag, contents not checked.
Chicago, Ill.

Al N. Miller   One brown billfold containing $85 in currency.
4827 West Oakdale
Chicago, Ill.

Bernard H. Voss   One zipper billfold containing $80 currency.

Charles Chamberlain One light brown billfold with identification
3229 Rose Ave   cards, no money.
Chicago, Ill.

Geo H. Whitney   One black billfold containing cards no cash.

Howard C. Stimpson   One brown imitation leather bag, locked.

Received

Signed _R. L. Carroll_____

Title _Asst Chf Spl. Agt_____

Address _Chicago_____

Page 2

INVESTIGATIONS OF RAILROAD ACCIDENTS 1911 - 1993

File Number	2988
Railroad	CHICAGO, BURLINGTON & QUINCY RAILROAD
Date	04/25/1946
Location	NAPERVILLE, IL.
Accident Type	R.E.

 Link to PDF Version

INTERSTATE COMMERCE COMMISSION

WASHINGTON

INVESTIGATION NO. 2988

CHICAGO, BURLINGTON & QUINCY RAILROAD COMPANY REPORT IN RE
ACCIDENT AT NAPERVILLE, ILL., ON APRIL 26, 1946

Inv-2988

SUMMARY

Railroad:	Chicago, Burlington & Quincy	
Date:	April 25, 1946	
Location:	Naperville, Ill.	
Kind of accident:	Rear-end collision	
Trains involved:	Passenger:	Passenger
Train numbers:	11:	39
Engine numbers:	Diesel-electric units 9920 A and 9920 B:	
	Diesel-electric units 9910 A and 9910 B	
Consist:	13 cars:	9 cars
Estimated speed:	Standing:	45 m.p.h.

114

Operation:	Signal indications
Tracks: westward	Three; tangent; 0.24 percent descending grade
Weather:	Clear
Time:	1:05 p.m.
Casualties:	45 killed; 69 injured
Cause: with cars meeting	Failure to operate following train in accordance with signal indications

Recommendation: That the Chicago, Burlington & Quincy Railroad Company   discontinue the operation of passenger train cars which do not meet present standards, intermingled in trains with cars meeting   such standards

Consideration of method for controlling speed deferred pending disposition of Docket No. 29543

INTERSTATE COMMERCE COMMISSION

INVESTIGATION NO. 2988

IN THE MATTER OF MAKING ACCIDENT INVESTIGATION REPOTS UNDER THE ACCIDENT REPORTS ACT CF MAY 6, 1910.

CHICAGO BURLINGTON & QUINCY RAILROAD COMPANY

July 30, 1946.

Accident at Naperville, Ill., on April 25, 1946, caused by failure to operate the following train in accordance with signal indications.

REPORT OF THE COMMISSION 1

PATTERSON, Commissioner:

On April 25, 1946, there were a rear-end collision between two passenger trains on the Chicago, Burlington & Quincy Railroad at Naperville, Ill., which resulted in the death of 39 passengers, 4 dinning-car employees, 1 employee off duty and 1 train-service employee, and the injury of 48 passengers, 1 porter, 19 dining-car employees and 1 train service employee. This accident was investigated in conjunction with representatives of the Illinois Commerce Commission.

Diagram

Inv. No. 2988 Chicago, Burlington & Quincy Railroad Naperville, Ill. April 25, 1946.

Location of Accident and Method of Operation

This accident occurred on that part, of the Chicago Division extending between Roosevelt

Road, Chicago, and Eola, Ill., 32 57 miles, a three-track line in the vicinity of the point of accident. The main tracks are designated from north to south as Nos. 1, 2 and 3. Trains moving in either direction on tracks Nos. 1 and 2 and east-bound trains moving on track No. 3 are operated by signal indications. The accident occurred on track No. 2 at a point 1,097 feet east of the station at Naperville, 26.94 miles west of Roosevelt Road. From the east there are, in succession, a tangent 4,732 feet in length, a compound curve to the right 4,160 feet, the maximum curvature of which is 0 degree 49.12', and a tangent 1,850 feet to the point of accident and 4.20 miles westward. The grade for west-bound trains on track No. 2 varies between 0.014 and 0.10 percent descending 3,400 feet, practically level 1,900 feet, 0.60 percent ascending about 1,800 feet, then it varies between 0.11 and 0.27 percent descending 1,813 feet to the point of accident, where it is

0.24 percent.

Automatic signals 227.1 and 228.1, governing west-bound movements on track No. 2, are mounted on signal bridges located, respectively, 6,581 feet and 934 feet east of the point of accident. These signals are of the three-indication, color-light type, and are continuously lighted. The yellow aspect of signal 227 1 is 27 41 feet above the level of the tops of the rails and 3.53 feet north of the center-line of track No. 2. The red aspect of signal 228.1 is 21.89 feet above the level of the tops of the rails and 6.5 feet north of the center-line of track No. 2. The involved aspects and corresponding indications and names of these signals are as follows:

Signal Name	Aspect	Indication
227.1 NEXT SIGNAL Approach-Signal	Yellow	APPROACH
	PREPARED TO STOP	
228.1 PROCEED Stop and Proceed Signal	Red	STOP; THEN

The controlling circuits of these signals are so arranged that, when a train is occupying track No. 2 in the block between signal 228.1 and the next signal westward, signal 227.1 displays approach-next-signal-prepared-to-stop, and signal 228.1 displays stop-then-proceed.

Operating rules read in part as follows:

DEFINITIONS

* * *

Restricted Speed. --Proceed prepared to stop snort of train, obstruction, or anything that may require the speed of a train to be reduced.

11.   A train finding a fusee burning op or near its track must stop and extinguish the fusee, and then proceed at restricted speed.

14.   ENGINE WHISTLE SIGNALS.

Note. --The signals prescribed are illustrated by "o" for short sounds; "--" for loaner sounds.

* * *

* * *

(c) ----- o o o   Flagman protect rear of train.

* * *

35.   The following signals will be used by flagmen:

Day signals-A red flag, Torpedoes and Fusees.

* * *

99.   When a train stops under circumstances in which
it may be overtaken by another train, the flagman must go back immediately with
flagman's signals a sufficient distance to insure full protection, placing two torpedoes, and
when necessary, in addition, displaying lighted fusses.

* * *

When a train is moving under circumstances in which it may be overtaken by another
train, the flagman must take such action as may be necessary to insure full protection. 3
night, or by day when the view is obscured, lighted fusees must be thrown off at proper
intervals.

* * *

509.   ***

* * *

When a train is stopped by a Stop and Proceed-signal it may proceed-

* * *

(B)   On two or more tracks at once at restricted
speed, expecting to find a train in the block, broken rail, obstruction or switch not
properly lined.

Time-table special instructions read in part as follows:

1.   When a distant signal is displaying a restricting
indication, trains must reduce speed at once and move at "restricted speed" until the
indication of the next governing signal can be determined.

37.   * * *

* * *

EMERGENCY RED REAR END LIGHTS. Trainmen on trains equipped with oscillating emergency red rear end lights must familiarize themselves with the location of the switches which control the lights and will be governed by the following.

* * *

To provide supplemental protection under Rule 99 in all circumstances where its use is necessary to stop following trains on one or more tracks.

* * *

The use of this emergency red light does not in any way relieve the flagman from flagman from full compliance with Rules 99. * * *.

* * *

The maximum authorized speed for the passenger trains involved was 80 miles per hour.

Description of Accident

No. 11, a west-bound first-class passenger train, consisted of Diesel-electric units 9920 A and 9920 B, one baggage car, one storage-mail car, two baggage cars, one mail car, one refrigerator-express car, two baggage cars, two coaches, one dining car, one parlor-lounge car and one, coach, in the order named. The sixth car was of steel-underframe construction, the ninth to eleventh-cars, inclusive, were of lightweight stainless-steel construction, and the remainder of the cars were of conventional all-steel construction. This train departed from Chicago Union Station, 28.44 miles east of Naperville, at 12:35 p.m., on time, and, moving on track No. 2, passed Downer's Grove, the last open office, 7.32 miles east of Naperville, at 12:57 p.m., 1 minute late. Soon afterward, some object was seen flying front beneath one of the cars and the train was stopped at Naperville for inspection at 1:03 p.m., with the rear end standing 1,097 feet east of the station. About 2 minutes later the rear end was struck by No. 39.

No. 39, a west-bound first-class passenger train, consisted of Diesel-electric units 9910 A and 9910 B, coupled in multiple control, three coaches, one dining car, two tourist sleeping cars and three Pullman sleeping cars, in the order named. All cars were of steel construction. This train departed from Chicago Union Station at 12:35 p.m., on time, and moved on track No. 1 to Kedzie Avenue, 23.59 miles east of Naperville, then entered track No. 2, passed Downer's Grove at 1 p.m., 2 minutes late, passed signal 227.1, which displayed approach-next-signal-prepared-to-stop, passed signal 228.1, which displayed stop-then-proceed, passed the flagman of No. 11, and while moving at an estimated speed of not less than 45 miles per hour it collided with No. 11 at a point 934 feet west of signal 228.1.

The ninth car of No. 11 was derailed and leaned to the south at an angle of 15 degrees, but remained in line with track No. 2. The center-sill was twisted and the roof sheets and the end sheets were somewhat damaged. The tenth car stopped on its left side south of track No. 2 and at an angle of 15 degrees to it. Both ends were buckled, the center-sill and cross members were bent, both draft gears were broken and both trucks were damaged. The eleventh car was turned around, bent into an U-shape, stopped north of the tenth car and against it, and was demolished about three-fourths of its length. The knuckle of the front coupler and the shank of the rear coupler were broken. The twelfth car was derailed across track No. 1 and stopped with its front end about 10 feet west of the tenth car and leaned to the north at an angle of 25 degrees. Both draft gears were broken, and both trucks were badly damaged. The front unit of engine 9910 entered the rear car of No. 11 above the floor-line and demolished the superstructure of this car about three-fourths its length. This car remained upright on track No. 2, and at the rear of the eleventh and twelfth cars The center-sill at the rear end was bent downward about 18 inches; the bend extended to the rear bolster. Both units of Diesel-electric engine 9910, of No. 39, were derailed but remained upright and in line with track No. 2. The front unit of this engine stopped inside the rear car No. 11 at a point 205 feet west of the point of collision. The front truck was torn off and stopped 18 feet west of the point of collision. The frames, the trucks, and the electrical and air equipment of both units were badly damaged. The first to fourth cars, inclusive, and the rear truck of the fifth car of No. 39 were derailed. This equipment remained, upright and in line with track No. 2. The rear end of the second car telescoped the front end of the third car about 6 feet. The derailed cars of No. 39 were damaged, but not extensively.

The weather was clear at the time of the accident, which occurred about 1:05 p.m.

The fireman of No. 39, who jumped from the engine just before the collision occurred, was killed. The engineer of No. 39 was injured.

According to data furnished by the railroad, the weight of the equipment of No, 39 was 1,043.04 tons. The ninth to eleventh cars, inclusive, of No. 11 were of lightweight stainless-steel construction. The twelfth and thirteenth cars of No. 11 were of conventional all-steel, plate, girder, post and sill construction. The ninth and tenth cars were built in 1940, the eleventh car, in 1938, and the twelfth and thirteenth cars, in 1918.

Diesel-electric engine 9910 is provided with M-40-A brake equipment. A safety-control feature is so arranged that when there is no pressure exerted or either the foot pedal or the automatic brake-valve handle, the train brakes will be applied in emergency, unless a brake application of 30 pounds brake-cylinder pressure has been made. To apply the train-brake system in emergency by manual operation, the brake-valve handle must be moved to the extreme right of the brake-valve quadrant. The equipment is so arranged that during an emergency application of the brakes sand is automatically deposited upon the rails. The regulating devices were adjusted for brake-pipe pressure of 110 pounds and main-reservoir pressure of 140 pounds. Of the cars of No. 39, four were equipped with UC-12-3 control valves, and five with LN-3 control valves. Both units of the Diesel-electric engine and 6 cars were equipped with clasp brakes, and the other cars were equipped with one brake shoe per wheel.

After the accident, tests of the air-brake equipment of No. 39 disclosed that the automatic brake valve and all control valves of the units involved functioned as intended, both in service and in emergency applications. The brake-cylinder piston travel of the nine cars varied between 6-1/2 and 9-1/4 inches. The piston travel of one car only was in excess of 9 inches.

A few days after the accident a series of braking tests was conducted with a train comparable in weight, braking ratios, and consist to that of No. 39 on the day of the accident. During one test a speed of 81 miles per hour was attained and a 30-pound brake-pipe reduction, which was initiated at signal 227.1, stopped the train at a point 33 feet east of signal 228.1. During the next test, a speed of 85 miles per hour was attained and a 30-pound brake-pipe reduction, which was initiated at signal 227.1, stopped the train at a point 33 feet east of signal 228.1. During another test, an emergency application made at a point 2.202 feet east of signal can be obtained, stopped the train from a speed of 86 miles per hour in a distance of 3,529 feet, at a point 1,327 feet west of signal 228.1 and 393 feet west of the point of accident.

Discussion

As No. 11 approaching Naperville, the speed was about 80 miles per hour. The front brakeman, who was making a running inspection of his train from the right rear vestibule of the tenth car, saw an unidentified object fly from under the train, and soon afterward sounded the communicating system signal to stop. The train was stopped 1-1/2 miles westward about 1:03 p.m., in the vicinity of the station at Naperville, with the rear end standing 1,850 feet west of the west end of a 0 degree 49.12'-curve to the right and 934 feet west of automatic signal 228.1. About 2 minutes later the rear end of No. 11 was struck by No. 39. At this time the train brakes of No. 11 were released; but the brakes on both Diesel-units were applied.

As No. 11 was approaching Naperville the flagman was stationed in the front end of the twelfth car, so that he could inspect his train as it moved on the curve to the right. His flagging equipment was on the rear platform of the rear or thirteenth car. When the flagman felt the application of the brakes as his train was preparing to stop at Naperville he proceeded to the rear end of the train and, after No. 11 stopped, he proceeded to the rear to provide flag protection. He had reached a point about 300 feet to the rear of his train and was giving stop signals with a red flag ten the engine of No. 39 passed him. He said that he was unable to make an inspection of his train from any point to the rear of the front end of the twelfth car, because of the type of equipment involved. It had been his experience that fusees dropped from a train moving at high speed would not remain lighted, and for this reason he said it had not been his practice to drop lighted fusees from a moving train. In tests after the accident, lighted 10-minute fusees were dropped from the rear Platform of a train moving on track No. 2. At speeds in excess of 40 miles per hour, fusees either bounced off track No. 2 or failed to burn. Burning fusees remained on track No. when dropped at speeds of 40 miles per hour and lower and continued to burn. The engineer of No. 11 said that he did not sound the engine-whistle signal for the flagman to protect the rear of the train until his train had stopped. The flagman proceeded to the rear immediately to provide flag protection. He did not operate the switch to light the oscillating red light which was provided at the rear of the train for giving additional waning. This device was therefore not operating. The sun was shining and, because of the curvature of track to the rear of No. 11, there is some question whether the engineer of No. 39 could have seen the oscillating red light, had it been lighted, in time to take action to stop his train short of the preceding train.

As No. 39 was approaching Naperville, the speed was about 80 miles per hour. Both enginemen were in the control compartment at the front end of the first Diesel-electric unit, and the members of the train crew were in various locations throughout the cars of the train, the engineer was seriously injured in the accident and he was unable to make a statement before this investigation was completed. The fireman jumped from the control compartment of the first Diesel-electric unit just before the, impact occurred, end he was killed. Members of the train crew were not aware that anything was wrong until the collision occurred. Several members of the train crew said they felt a light service application of the brakes about midway between signals 227.1 and 228.1. Those employees thought the speed was about 45 miles per hour at the time of the collision. The brakes of this train had been tested and had functioned properly en route. In tests of the brake equipment of this train after the accident, the brakes functioned properly in both service and emergency applications and the brake-cylinder piston travel was in conformity with the requirements. The automatic sanding feature of the Diesel-electric units functioned during emergency application of the brakes after the accident.

Signal 227.1 displayed approach for No 39. Under the rules this indication required the train to "approach next signal prepared to stop." On most railroads the indication for an approach signal is "Proceed preparing to stop at next signal. Train exceeding medium speed must at once reduce to that speed." This latter indication establishes a definite minimum requirement which is essential to safe operation and which if it had been followed in this case would have prevented this accident. On the Chicago, Burlington & Quincy Railroad the approach indication is supplemented by a time-table instruction which provides that when a distant signal is displaying a restricting indication, trains must reduce seed at once and move at restricted speed until the indication of the next governing signal can be determined. Under this instruction, as soon as the approach aspect of signal 227.1 came into view the speed of No. 39 should have been reduced at once, and the train should have proceeded prepared to stop short of train, obstruction or anything that the restricted speed indication was protecting. Had the signal been observed and this instruction complied with, this accident would have been prevented. Signal 228.1 displayed stop-then-proceed, which indication required that the train must be stooped and then operated beyond this signal in such manner that it could be stooped short of a preceding train. The weather was clear and there was no condition which obscured the view of the aspects displayed by signals 227.1 and 228.1. Signal 227.1 could be seen from the control compartment of No. 39 throughout a distance of not less than 5,000 feet. In tests after the accident signals 227.1 and 228.1 functioned properly. Examination of Diesel-electric engine 9910 after the accident disclosed that the automatic brake valve was in service position. There was no indication that an emergency application of the brakes had been made. The members of the train crew of No. 39 said that they did not feel any brake application in the vicinity of aperville until their train was midway between signals 227.1 and 228.1. A series of braking tests was conducted after the accident, with a train of similar weight and brake system to No. 39 on the day of the accident. As a result of 30-pound service brake-pipe reductions made at signal 227.1, the test train stopped from speeds of 80 and 85 miles per hour short of signal 228.1. Since it was not possible to question the engineer of No. 39 during this investigation, it is not known why action was not taken by him to operate No. 39 in accordance with the indications displayed by the signals involved

According to the timetable in effect at the time of the accident, the scheduled leaving time from Chicago Union Station for Nos. 11 and 39 was 12:35 p.m. The leaving time for No. 11 from Downer's Grove, 7.32 miles east of Naperville, was 12:56 p.m., and for No. 39, 12:58 p.m. This was close headway. In the operation of trains under such headway engineers should be especially alert at all times. In a new timetable, effective May 26, 1946, the scheduled leaving time from Chicago Union Station for No. 11 is 12:30 p.m., and for No. 39, 12:45 p.m., which provides at all times. In a new timetable, effective May 26, 1946, the scheduled leaving time from Chicago Union Station for No. 11 is 12:30 p.m., and for No. 39, 12:45 p.m., which provides a time interval of 15 minutes. However, increased of the time interval between these schedules will riot necessarily prevent similar accidents, because trains scheduled 15 or more minutes apart at their initial terminal can close up until a situation develops similar to the one involved in the accident here under investigation. If an adequate automatic train-stop or train-control system had been in use end functioning properly, the speed of No. 39 would have been controlled in accordance with the conditions of track occupancy ahead, regardless of any inaction on the part of the engineer, and this accident would have been averted. If a cab-signal system had been in use and functioning properly, an audible warning signal would have been sounded, and signal aspects indicating the presence of the train ahead would have been displayed continuously in the cab in the view of both the engineer and the fireman, and this accident might have been averted.

There is now pending before the Commission docket No. 29543, which is an investigation instituted May 20, 1946, on its own motion, to determine whether it is necessary, in the public interest, to require any common carrier by railroad to install block signal system, interlocking, automatic train stop, train control and/or cab signal devices, and/or other similar appliances, methods and systems intended to promote the safety of railroad operation, upon the whole or any part of its railroad on which any train is operated at a speed of 50 or more miles per hour. Hearing therein will be held in the near future.

The thirteenth or rear car of No. 11 was of conventional all-steel construction, and weighed 10,300 pounds. As a result of direct shock in the collision, the center-sills were bent downward about 18 inches at the rear end, and the bend extended to the rear bolster. The first unit of the locomotive of No. 39 was deflected upward; it entered the rear car above the floor level, and the superstructure was destroyed about three-fourths the length of the car. As a result of the upward deflection of the first unit of the locomotive, the buffing members of the rear car did not receive the full force of the collision. A considerable amount of the force was dissipated in the twelfth, eleventh, tenth and ninth cars. The greatest damage and practically all the deaths occurred in the thirteenth and eleventh cars. The twelfth car was of conventions all-steel construction, and weighed 169,800 pounds. It was not damaged extensively. The eleventh, tenth and ninth cars were of lightweight construction; and weighed, respectively, 115,800, 112,950, and 110,700 pounds. The eighth and seventh cars were of conventional all-steel construction, and weighed, respectively, 139,700 and 141,800 pounds. The eleventh car stopped in reverse direction. It was bent in an U-shape. The section between the body bolsters was demolished, and the sections between the body bolsters and the ends were considerably damaged. The eleventh, tenth and ninth cars were equipped with tightlock couplers.

Examination of the extent of damage to each of the rear five cars of No. 11 directs attention to the comparative capacities of these cars to withstand heavy buffing stresses. Specifications for end-to-end buffing stresses for passenger-train cars were first promulgated In 1912 for railway post office cars. These specifications required that such cars must be constructed so as to resist buffing stress of not less than 800,000 pounds, and this requirement has not been changed. In 1939, the Association of American Railroads recommended to its members certain specifications, based on the existing Railway Mail Service specifications, for the construction of passenger cars used in trains of more than 600,000 pounds light weight. Those specifications, made standard by the Association of American Railroads in 1945, require that the car structure resist minimum static end load of 800,000 pounds applied on center line of draft without developing any permanent deformation in any member of the car structure. The eleventh car was a dining car built in 1938, and was of stainless steel construction. The center-sill of this car was of stainless steel, with a cross-sectional area of 8.38 square inches. This is insufficient to meet the specifications recommended by the Association of American Railroads in 1939 and made standard by it in 1945. In recent years similar cars have boon constructed with stainless steel center-sills having a cross-sectional area of 18 square inches. The cross-sectional areas of the center-sills of the tenth and ninth cars were about 40 percent greater than that of the eleventh car. Several railroads have in use a total of about 105 cars of the same specifications as the eleventh car in No. 11, and about 20 of these are in use by the Chicago, Burlington & Quincy Railroad.

In 1938 the Commission investigated a head-end collision between two passenger trains in which there were cars of similar specifications to that of the dinning car of No. 11. In that accident as well as the present one, the first car of such specifications in the line of travel of the force of collision received far greater damage than the adjoining cars which were of heavier construction. In both cases there were cars of heavier construction beyond the cars in question, and they received only minor damage.

The following recommendation was made in the Commission's report covering investigation of this 198 accident:

It is recommended that railroad officials give serious consideration to discontinuance of operation, of so-called lightweight cars between or ahead of standard, cars unless and until the strength of construction has been determined by suitable tests to be substantially the same as that of other cars with which they are associated.

Notwithstanding this recommendation, and also the subsequent action of the Association of American Railroads establishing a minimum requirement of resistance to end buffing stresses for cars in unrestricted service, cars which do not conform to this standard are continued in operation in association with cars of substantially heavier construction and which meet this minimum requirement. The number of casualties which resulted in this case may have been attributable in part to this condition. Only the three lightweight cars were equipped with tightlock couplers. Had all the cars involved been equipped with tightlock couplers, and had all cars conformed to the standard for end buffing resistance, it is probable that the disastrous consequences of this accident would have been greatly reduced.

Cause

It is found that this accident was caused by failure to operate the following train in accordance with signal indications.

Recommendation

It is recommended that the Chicago, Burlington & Quincy Railroad Company discontinue the operation of passenger-train cars which do not meet present standards, intermingled in trains with cars meeting such standards.

No recommendation is made at this time with respect to the method of controlling the speed of these fast trains, since this matter is receiving comprehensive consideration in our docket No. 29543.

Dated at Washington, D. C., this thirtieth day of July, 1946.

By the Commission, Commissioner Patterson.

W. P. BARTEL,

(SEAL)

Secretary.

FOOTNOTE:

1   Under authority of section 17 (2 of the Interstate Commerce Act the above-entitled proceeding was referred by the Commission to Commissioner Patterson for consideration and disposition.

ACKNOWLEDGMENTS

Michal Adelman, Jeanne Clemens Aeby, Holly Whittet-Allison, David Alstadt, Terry Altheide, James Ballowe, Sharon Barnett, Barbara Bates, Jim and Diane Bauer, George Becker, Mary Bellis, Marvin Bensema, Brand Bobosky, Dr. Mary Ann Bobosky, Debra Bolda, Tonya Boltz, Ann Brown, Ken Bauder, Jim Bauer, JoAnn Martin Baumgartner, Stu Beitler, Marvin Bensema, Bob and Bee Bremmer, Holly Burgess, Kim Jacobson Butler, Karen Campbell, Britt Carson, Marilyn Cawiezel, Larry Cena, Monique Ciofu, Fran Clark, Jacob Cleary, Carol Lee Schrader Cole, Brad Cook, William Cronin, Dorian Davis, Margo Davis, Dick Dearborn, Donna DeFalco, Lorna Donley, Monsignor Jos. Dowdell, Nancy Drago, Heidi Selzler-Echola, Jane Easterly, Clyde Erwin, Carolyn Lauing Finzer, Spike Flanders, Kevin Frantz, Helen Fraser, Lynn Freisner, Angela Gates, Kathy Gerling, Daniel Glauber, Raymond Grabowski, Jr., James R. Grossman, Kim Grouper, Vivian Hall, Rick Haase, Trish Hard, Rita Fredenhagen Harvard, Rodney Harvey, Dawn Hayslett, Barbara Widder Heintz, Samantha Helmick, Ken and Elaine Hess, Henry Wayland Hill, Arnie and Kaye Hodel, Hogan's Hut Breakfast Bunch, Travis Huffman, Larry Huto, Raymond Jaeger Jr., Bev Johnson, Ken Kane, Ann Keating, Ron Keller, Maxwell Kerr, Brandon and Danielle Kessler, Kim King, Marion Knoblauch, Paul Kostansek, Charles Ladd, Ralph Landorf, Carol Lefteroff, Craig Lefteroff, Tiffany Lucashefski, Marty and Mary Lou Lydecker, Jim Mabus, Rolla Martin, Joan Masat, Philip Mason, Roger Matile, Boyd and Mary Lou Matteson, Linda Maxton, Ryan Maxwell, Jack McCarthy, Stephen McGrath, Shannon McGregor, Carol Meisenheimer, John Wayne Miller, Lou Ann Moore, Jean Morris, Patty Mosher, Sheila Mosley, Rick and Ginni Nelson, Dave Newman, Henry Neyra, Bill Oddo, Blaine Overman, Linda Overman, Richard C. Overton, Dr. Ted and Mary Parran, Stephanie Penick, Craig and Cheryl Phillips, Susan Ponce, Jerry Pottebaum, Lorilyn Rackl, Mary Ramm, Al and Pat Rechenmacher, Helen Rechenmacher, Joe and Esther Rechenmacher, Helene Rehs, Janice Reiff, Jim Reisdorff, Paul Rickert, Jim Roselle, Jana Rowe, Martha Russell, Bope Schrader, Harold Schrader, David Schau, Bill Seiser, Beth Sheffer, Sue Shidler, Al, Laurie, and Sara Siebert, Bob and Kathy Spinner, Gertrude Spinner, John and Katy Spinner, Edward F. Streit Jr., Jennifer Streff, Debbie Sargent-Sullivan, Lynn Sullivan, Virginia Supik, James Svehla, Russell Swirin, Summer Thomas, David Thompson, Kathy Thornton, Al and Mary Ann Toenjes, Patricia Tomczak, Fred Tavakovi, Genevieve Towsley, Carol VanValkenburg, Karen VanValkenburg, Sister Janet Voss, Paul Walker, Joan Weis, Calista Wehrli, Janet Wehrli, Tim West, Daniel Wewers, Beverly Whitaker, Edith Widder, Rick Willman, Traci Williams, Traci Wilson, Bill Wood, Julie Wullner, David Young, Malea Young, Chuck Zeiler, Rose Mary Chepon, John Boyajiari, Bob Fieseler, Judi Goerke, J.R. Turner, Marilyn and Steve Wozneak, Jeff Malick, Amanda Warren, Lou Lalonde, Tom Lalonde, Chris Bienio, Debbie Pusback, Sister deLourdes Rechenmacher, and to all the people I somehow forgot to list but who gave help and support along the way.